# BUILDING CHAMPIONS:

## A GUIDE FOR PARENTS
## OF JUNIOR GOLFERS

**Dr. Bee Epstein-Shepherd**

**BECOMING PRESS**
Box 221383
Carmel, California, 93922

For information on special discounts for non-profit organizations or bulk purchases, contact the publisher above.

Book Design: Valley Typesetters, Carmel Valley, California
Printed in the United States of America

Library of Congress Control Number 2005901994
ISBN 0-9616204-6-3
First Edition, 10 9 8 7 6 5 4 3 2 1

**This book is lovingly dedicated to my grandchildren:**

✦ Jacob Moss,

✦ Grayson, Weston and Drake Epstein,

✦ Nicholas Kelly, and his soon to be born twin sisters

✦ The Shepherd kids, Steven, Daniel, Matthew and Amy

✦ and the Perry boys, Robbie, Tyler, Spencer and Austin

I am grateful for Bettina, Nicole and Seth who turned out to be admirable human beings in spite of my inexperience and mistakes when they were children. I am thankful that they chose wonderful spouses in Richard, Mike, and Monica, and that they are raising amazing children to be champion human beings. I add gratitude that Bob and Tami, and Sharon and Chuck have accepted me into their clan so completely.

## Acknowledgements:

I sit in solitude at the computer, totally immersed in producing this book. Though writing can be a solitary activity, it comes only after inspiration from and collaboration with others. I acknowledge and thank those who generously gave time and honest answers when I interviewed them. Some are mentioned by name in the book. I interviewed too many to name them all here. This book would not have been written were it not for Erik Eidsmo, who suggested it several years ago, and then offered help and resources all along the way. Many golf writers gave me the benefit of their years of insights into aspects of professional golf that are not apparent to the fans. Thanks to Jay Coffin, Jaime Diaz, Lance Ringler, Jeff Rude, Ron Sirak, John Strege and Ed Vyeda, who at first was a resource and then my editor, and to T.R. Reinman who gave me valuable information and contacts. I must also thank the professional golfers who have trusted me with their mental games and allowed me into their private lives. Finally to all my clients who have probably taught me as much as I have taught them. This is definitely a team effort.

# TABLE OF CONTENTS

# INTRODUCTION

*If raising children was going to be easy, it wouldn't have started with something called LABOR.* – Dr. Bee

In the summer of 2001, Erik Eidsmo, the father of Bentley, one of my junior clients, said, "There is no simple advice or guidelines available for parents whose children play golf competitively." He had asked me for advice on how to encourage his son without being overbearing. "At junior tournaments," he said, "I've noticed some parents are far more actively involved in their kid's game than others." What he meant by "actively involved" was really "domineering."

Bentley's parents were investing time and money in golf lessons, tournament fees and in what is unusual for juniors, my services as mental skills coach. Erik wanted to provide his son with every opportunity, yet avoid pushing or pressuring him. I had no concerns for Erik, or Bentley, because any conversation we had revolved around, "How can I be a better parent?" So many other parents focus on, "What do I have to do to fix my child?"

When Erik suggested I write a book for parents, I thought the idea was interesting, but I was busy working with clients and was still developing the *"Mental Mastery System"* as a follow-up to my book, *"Mental Management for Great Golf,"* so the idea was shelved. Later that year one of my clients who had won a championship on the Japan LPGA tour went to the LPGA Tour Qualifying School in an attempt to earn playing privileges in the United States. She shot in the 80s and eliminated herself early in the process. Afterward, she told me her father had made an unexpected appearance at the tournament and she felt so much pressure from him that she couldn't play well.

Pressure from parents – almost always from fathers – that leads to anxiety on the golf course had been a constant theme with junior, amateur and professional clients having performance problems. I began to pay more attention to the influence of parental behavior on performance. I also have been working with the families of golfers, helping them deal with the long-term consequences of over-enthusiastic parental involvements (also called "domination.") It is obvious that parenting behavior has a huge impact on emotional and mental health – and for golfers, ultimate performance in competition and in life satisfaction.

After several years of experience with both junior and adult golfers dealing with the negative effects of parental pressure, I decided that the time had come. I am well aware that there is good and bad parenting in all sports, but since 95 percent of my clients are golfers, this book focuses on golf. However, anyone can use these principles to guide children who play baseball, soccer, or tennis, or compete in skating, riding, swimming and gymnastics. The basic principles apply equally to the school and home environments. Change a word or two and you can build champion athletes, scholars and champion human beings.

♛

**My bias is that your first priority as a parent is to build a champion human being. In this arena, no competition is involved. Every child is born with championship potential. For golfers, trophies, college scholarships and even a pro career can be welcome bonuses.**

There is no formula for perfect parenting. Let's take an analogy: if there were such a thing as a perfect golfer, he would regularly score in the 50s. Obviously, no golfer is a perfect; as a matter of fact, only six professionals have shot as low as 59 in official competition. And these golfers have only done that once each– so far.

Contemporary stars like Tiger Woods, Annika Sorenstam, Ernie Els and Phil Mickelson, as well as "classic" champions like Jack Nicklaus, Arnold Palmer, Ben Hogan and Kathy Whitworth, all have made many mistakes on their way to plentiful victories, including numerous major championships. Their wins are a result of recovering from and learning from mistakes. **Parents will "win" by recovering from and learning from mistakes – and not repeating them.**

> *"You can't learn from a mistake you*
> *don't admit you made."*
> — Hayes McClerkin

♛

You already have done much right in the parenting arena. Yet no matter what you do and how hard you try, it is inevitable that sometimes you will "blow it." Most mistakes are easily remedied, while others take extensive therapy to fix. There are even those mistakes that can waste a life. If you follow the guidelines in this book, you will avoid serious mistakes and make only those that can be easily remedied. This book gives you general principles that work. There are always exceptions. There are kids whose parents did everything "right" who still turn out troubled. There are kids who come from the most disadvantaged environments, yet have the drive to make the most of their lives and become exceptional human beings.

♛

It is my intention that each short section in this book

stimulates thinking. Some sections will strike you as, "Ho hum, of course I knew that." That's because you are the kind of parent who will see yourself in a lot of the positive examples. Hopefully, the negative examples that you can relate to will cause you to seriously examine your behavior. You may recognize that you are pushing your child too hard, expecting too much, either in golf or at school, or both. You might discover that your communication style causes your child to "click off" when you start to talk to him. You may see that your sacrifices are one-sided and it is time to expect more from your child, or that discipline is lacking in your home.

This book will give you insights, things to think about, ways to examine your behavior. Decide to work on specific changes in your behavior and in your home that will build a "champion family." I will suggest "How To Do It" references. The very best comprehensive book on parenting I have found is Dr. Phil McGraw's recent work, *"Family First."* Read it; take it to heart. The more you learn, the better equipped you will be to become champion parents, raising champion children.

♛

Part I gives you my definition and concept of a champion. Junior golfers will identify parental behaviors that interfere with performance and things their parents do that are helpful. You will get the chance to evaluate yourself. You will learn about parenting styles and behaviors that are the most likely to result in happy kids who love playing golf and who turn out to be good human beings.

Part II discusses the three basic principles for building champions:

✦ Principle #1: Love your child unconditionally.

◆ Principle #2: Support your child in achieving his dreams.

◆ Principle #3: Teach your child to live responsibly.

You will be reminded of things a child must learn in order to live a satisfying, productive life.

Part III explores vital topics such as motivation, listening, criticism, discipline, lessons and tournaments with ideas for constructively handling issues that parents and golfing kids deal with on a daily basis.

In Part IV professionals give advice based on their experience coaching kids. It's interesting that their comments are so consistent: "Make golf fun," "Don't push or pressure," and, "Stay out of the way."

In Part V you will learn techniques for building self-esteem in your child, an essential element in peak performance. Jack Nicklaus said golf is 90 percent mental. Tiger Woods' upbringing and training is a demonstration of that belief. You are introduced to the relationship between the mind and body and mental training techniques that round out your child's performance repertoire.

If you learn only one constructive thing by reading this book and you apply that to your child or family, you will be headed in the right direction. You can compare it to making one small adjustment in alignment on the tee that keeps the ball in the fairway. Each section has something to consider or learn that is comparable to that small adjustment in alignment.

♛

I'll be telling many stories. Most of these stories and examples come from my experience with players and parents, but I will indicate examples gathered from the media and credit information offered from other experts. I will use real names only when people's behavior is admirable and if I have permission. If behavior is not admirable, or if I feel it is important to protect the name of a player, or family, I will not use real names. Sometimes examples will be combined, again to protect the identity of the player and parents.

Each section ends with an Action Idea: it might be an evaluation tool, a game to introduce into your household, or just a simple idea to try. Each will give you a way to take a constructive step on the way toward the goals of your child and family. It may be the one step that increases the chances that your child will be a champion in a champion family.

# PART I
## SETTING THE STAGE

*"Just offer the opportunity. Put the clubs in the corner and give them access to a place to play. That might mean driving them to a course, or just buying them a bicycle. Anything more than that and you can run the risk of turning off your children to a game they could enjoy their whole life..."*
– Nick Price, on how to be a golfing father

Marc O'Hair thought he had all the answers. He knew he was "right." A quick glance at the cover of the Jan. 19, 2005 issue of *GolfWeek* magazine appears to support him. His son Sean's face, dominating the cover, is above the caption: *"The Tour's Most Compelling Rookie"* followed in smaller print by, *"Sean O'Hair makes it to the big time – after a painful split with his iron-willed dad."*

The cover story is of a father's ambition gone awry. In 1999, Sean was a 17-year-old American Junior Golf Association (AJGA) star who turned pro while still a junior in high school. He and his dad went on the road seeking their fortune on tour. Sean signed a contract with dad requiring him to pay dad 10 percent of his professional earnings for life. Dad told him, *"I can't blow this kind of money without a return ...when you make it there has to be payback someday."*

Sean is quoted as saying, *"We never had a father son-relationship. It has always been the investor and the investment. That's a tough deal when it comes to family, I basically felt like I was thrown to the wolves. ...the welfare of my family was on a 17-year-old's shoulders...I wasn't making any money at all, and we were putting lots of money into it."*

Sean finally had enough of his father's many years of heartless drill sergeant training tactics and abuse. He cut loose of dad's control at the age of 20. He married and then his fortunes turned. Helped by the loving support of his wife and in-laws, Sean began to make money on the mini-tours and at age 22 earned his PGA Tour card at his first Tour Qualifying School appearance at the end of 2004.

Sean's rise to golf's big stage is s a sad story of a misguided father imposing his will and harsh physical and emotional punishment on his talented golfer son. It is only one of many similar stories of broken relationships in golfing families. "But," the misguided parents might argue, "they are successful professionals on tour."

There are a number of golfers who have made it to the tour at a younger age than Sean O'Hair, who were raised by supportive, loving parents. You will meet some of them in later stories. And since you are reading this book, you are a parent who wants to do the best possible parenting job for your child. Armed with OPE (Other People's Experience) you can model your parenting after families that are intact and happy – champion families.

♛

# Definition: Champion

<u>American College Dictionary</u>: *1. One who holds first place in any sport, etc. having defeated all opponents. 2. Anything that takes first place in competition.*

<u>Dr. Bee</u>: *A person who fulfills his potential and lives a life of satisfaction and service.*

The dictionary definition deals only with winning in competition, a feat that generally earns a prize or trophy. My definition is more inclusive. I believe there are more things to win than a trophy. One can win friends, win the love of family, and win respect. Though a trophy-winner may have fulfilled his potential in one area, most people have potential that even they might not be aware of. The true champion has a life in addition to his sport and can find satisfaction in a variety of activities.

I have added service to my definition, because a true champion is part of the human race, not just a particular race to the top of his sport. Golf focuses on giving. So many professionals say that golf has given them so much, they want to give back to the sport. The Tiger Woods Foundation funnels millions of dollars to community based youth programs. In 2004, Phil Mickelson and Catherine Cartwright, a young LPGA Tour player, donated a sum for every birdie made during their tournaments to benefit the children of Special Operation Forces killed in the line of duty. Johnny Miller, who established the Johnny Miller Junior Golf Foundation, donates his time to junior clinics and other charitable events. A complete champion lives not only for his personal satisfaction, but makes giving or service part of his life. As you build a complete champion, the trophies become mere bonuses in a meaningful life

♛

When I work with junior golfers, I provide guidance to the parents. Some parents need no more than brief contact and updates, while others need extensive direction. It does no good to work on building confidence with a player if he goes home to a father who compares him unfavorably with his older brother, or other players, and continually points out his shortcomings. Many times I see my job as working mainly with the parents – to make sure that in their zeal to create the next Tiger, or Annika, they don't undermine the self-esteem of their vulnerable, sensitive child. Parents need to be clear that children have not matured physically, emotionally, or mentally. Children do not have "common sense," or understand the consequences of their actions at the adult level. Children must be taught patiently, and learn from making their own mistakes. I must often remind a parent, "Even though he is six feet tall and can bomb a ball 295 yards, he is only 15 years old. His mind and emotions have not kept up with his physical growth. You cannot expect him to think like a touring pro. Guiding children in effective age-appropriate ways will hasten the development of character and championship behavior.

♛

At age 5, Jordan was a fun-loving boy who was so enamored of Tiger Woods and golf that he had to be dragged off the course when it was time to eat or sleep. Jordan won a number of junior tournaments and became a "celebrity" when he hit a Velcro golf ball to the middle of a bullseye adhered to Tom Arnold's chest on the "The Best Damn Sports Show Period." Jordan's dad, Johnny, asked me to work on Jordan's "mental game." I have never believed a 5 year-old needs to work on his mental game. As a matter of fact, I don't believe any junior needs my help until he feels real pressure in competition. I used to say that age 13 or 14 was early enough to work with a mental skills coach, or sport psychologist. However, I now am very aware of the performance pressure being put on kids as young as 6. (The Junior World Championship now has a category for ages 6 and under). This pressure with the potential of eroding self-confidence can create serious problems later.

With that in mind, I am now willing to work with any age child – mainly to have access to the parents. I want to teach the parents how to provide the championship environment in a way that is age-appropriate. For example, the first thing I taught Jordan's father was to not use the term, "bad shot." When I walked with them during a tournament practice round, I heard Johnny tell Jordan, "That was a bad shot, you rushed it." I saw Jordan's troubled expression. A 5-year-old doesn't need criticism, and really doesn't know how to correct the error. He needs encouragement and information. I suggested that Dad use the term, "accident." As in, "Whoops that was an accident, next time look at where you want the ball to go and take your time before you hit it." Recently, Johnny told me that he modified what he learned from me on the golf course and applied it at home and at work. "I talk to people differently now and I get much better results from the people I train and manage," he said.

☖

I met Jay Haas at the inaugural First Tee Open at Pebble Beach, a unique Champions Tour event where talented juniors were partnered with the senior pros (age 50-older) for all three rounds of the tournament. Jay and his junior partner, 15-year-old Sydney Burlison, who is a client of mine, came in second. I talked to Jay about his experience raising his own champion kids. (That weekend, Jay's 22 year-old son Bill was competing in a PGA Tour event, playing on a sponsor's exemption. An all-American graduate from Wake Forest University, where he was the No. 1 player on the team, Bill was trying to earn his Tour card for the 2005 season.) Jay said, "I taught them respect for themselves and the game, about character and integrity. I love them and guide them. It's just common sense."

To which I responded, "If it is just common sense, why are so many parents out there yelling, insulting and even being physically abusive to their kids in public? Why are so many professionals choking, playing poorly under pressure and getting psychological therapy? If they were raised with common sense, love and guidance, why are so many golfers at odds with their parents?

Actually, Jay Haas' "common sense" is consistent with my perspective. His "common sense" did produce champions. But many parents have a different perspective of "common sense."

One such parent with a reputation for over control told me the secret to raising champion kids is to hold them tight – as he clenched his fist. This parent has one touring professional, as well as two rebellious golfers in his family. He considers the child who plays on the LPGA Tour positive proof of his methods. Based on my work with one of his other children, I know that he could have had more than one professional champion in the family. My client was actually more talented than her successful sibling, but she was constantly told, "You'll never amount to anything if you don't listen to your father." With a mind of her own, she was not as meek and pliable as her older sister. She felt rejected, as her father gave all his attention to the sister he could control. The rejection and rebellion sabotaged my client's potential. The emotional damage done during her formative years will take a great deal of effort to undo, as she has become depressed. Based on the father's training philosophy I wonder how happy or emotionally well adjusted the "successful" sister is, and also wonder how long the success will last.

♛

The Tiger Woods story has been told many times. Often Earl Woods was portrayed as the overbearing militaristic Green Beret who subjected his son to rigorous psychological training. I discussed *"Building Champions"* with writer

John Strege, who authored a biography of Tiger Woods in 1997. John and I talked about the conclusions I have drawn from my experiences and research. He said that his experience in the Woods home during numerous extensive interviews contradicted the portrayal of Earl Woods as overbearing, and confirmed my findings. **Champion children and peak performers who become emotionally healthy adults are not pressured, or pushed by their parents. They are not berated, harshly criticized or punished. Instead they are encouraged and given opportunities in a loving supportive environment.** The real Earl Woods is a parent to emulate. To him and Tiger's mother, Kultida, it was most important that Tiger be a good person.

**A parent's primary job is to raise a child with inner resources and self-esteem who has that, "I can do it," attitude. A secondary job is to provide the opportunities to develop the skills necessary to help the child achieve his or her goals.** Some parents are not able to provide many opportunities, but a child raised with love, who has inner resources, self-esteem, and a dream is capable of creating his own opportunities.

♛

## They're not finished yet

A child or adolescent is not a small version of an experienced adult. There's a reason rental car agencies don't rent to anyone younger than age 25. According to new research, the brain isn't fully developed until then. The rental car executives didn't know about the brain; they just looked at accident rates.

My older daughter is a licensed social worker and therapist who was trained in childhood and family dynamics, so

I was interested in her input. (I was also interested in her childhood memories of my parenting, both pros and cons. I discussed this topic with each of my children as I was writing this book,) My daughter's professional advice was that it is important to understand normal stages of development so parents don't expect more than their kids are developmentally capable of. She suggested the book, *"Yes, Your Teen is Crazy"* by Michael J. Bradley, Ed.D

In his comprehensive book, Bradley cites the work of Dr. Jay Giedd, chief of brain imaging in the child psychiatry branch at the National Institute of Mental Health. Since 1991, Giedd and his collaborators at UCLA, Harvard, The Montreal Neurological Institute and other institutions have used magnetic resonance imaging (MRI) to study the brains of 1,800 children as they developed. The research concludes that the brain continues developing until the early 20s. This is contrary to previous beliefs that the brain was a finished product by age 12. This new research shows that the part of the brain that includes substantial adult functions – such as planning, setting priorities, organizing thoughts, suppressing impulses and weighing the consequences of one's actions –   is the last to develop. When "raging hormones" are added to the mix, adolescent behavior becomes even more unpredictable. This research is discussed in detail in a Time Magazine lead article, *"What makes Teens Tick"* (May 10, 2004).

According to Dr. Bradley, Both *"the toddler and adolescent brain at times are unstable, dysfunctional and completely unpredictable. They both have just developed a bunch of brain circuits that may fire off unexpectedly. Also they both have neurologically deficient controls to moderate these impulses and to understand the likely outcomes of their actions.*

***"In adolescent children,"*** *he continues,* ***"the maddening behavior is just the result of mixed-up wiring that will***

*straighten out in time, if and only if we adults respond not with raging hurtful punishments, but with carefully crafted responses intended to calmly but firmly teach brain-challenged children to become functional adults."*

♔

## If you want information, ask questions

Many years ago when I was a practicing Industrial Psychologist, I had the opportunity to hear the eminent management consultant Peter Drucker speak on how to elicit peak performance from employees. He said, "Walk around your company and ask each of your people, 'What do I do that helps you?' Write the answer down on the back of an envelope. Then ask them, 'What do I do that hinders you?' And write that down. Then do more of the former and less of the latter." I have used that piece of advice since.

While compiling information for this book, I modified Drucker's idea. I asked juniors questions like, "What do your parents do that helps you perform your best?" "What do your parents do that interferes with your best play? " "What could your parents do that would make them better golf parents?" Even though many said, "My parents are great," they still had a suggestion or two for improvement. The most common response revolved around a shared perception, "They don't understand me, or how things are from my perspective." Where have you heard that before? Isn't that a recurrent complaint of one spouse about the other, between employee and boss, or student and teacher?

Good parents want to know how they are perceived by their children. Asking for their feedback is a wonderful way to open conversations, as long as it doesn't get into the defensive, or the, "If you would only clean up your room I wouldn't have to yell at you" mode. Learn from your child's comments and use them as a guide to adjust your behavior. This information can be a stimulus for the growth and development of all members of the family. It is amazing how differently behavior is perceived by the doer and the receiver. A parent might think he delivered a mild reprimand, but it can be taken as a huge rebuke by the child. An offhand tease can be interpreted literally, taken to heart and have a negative impact later.

As you read this book you will learn how you can turn criticism, or fault-finding into constructive suggestions. You will learn how to avoid the frustration and anger that often produces only stubborn resistance. You will learn to appreciate your child's unique way of relating to the world and support her efforts at excellence. You will be providing the foundation upon which to build your champion. It is never too late to modify behavior and improve parent/child relationships. I'm still alert to that possibility in my family.

♛

## "This interferes with my best play."

**Comments from kids:**

✦ "I don't need my parents to criticize and push me. I'm hard enough on myself."

✦ "They don't have to go over every mistake. I know what I did wrong and feel bad enough."

✦ "They are always reminding me of what I need to do, but I find myself resisting when they keep harping on stuff. (This comment also applied to cleaning their rooms. One said, "It's the only way I can rebel without hurting myself.)

✦ "Once I reached a certain level my mother expected me to play at that level all the time. She's not a golfer and doesn't realize you can't always shoot in the low 70s."

✦ "The first thing they focus on is my score. Sometimes when my score is bad, I feel have made progress with my course management, or controlling my emotions. I can be proud of myself for hanging in there and giving it my best until the end. But if the score isn't good, I get no acknowledgment for progress."

✦ "He thinks I don't know he's watching when he hides behind trees. I know he is there judging me. That's worse than if he were out in the open – then I wouldn't have to wonder where he was when I am playing." (On a lighter note, one junior said, "If he's going to hide behind trees, at least he shouldn't wear a red sweater!")

✦ "He criticizes shots in front of my friends. It's bad enough that he finds so much wrong. I wish he would wait till we're alone."

✦ "He's get so mad and yells at me when I hit a bad shot – I don't do it on purpose. If I don't play well he punishes me by grounding or not letting me do other stuff I like."

✦ "He always focuses on what I'm doing wrong – and he doesn't say it nicely. He calls me stupid. I wish he wouldn't ask why I made that mistake – I don't know. If I knew I wouldn't make it."

* "He says the score isn't the most important thing, but that's all he talks about and I always see him taking notes. Sometimes I wonder what he's writing down. That distracts my focus."

* "He expects me to stay cool, but he blows up himself."

* "He's loud and embarrasses me in front of everybody."

* "I'm afraid of my parents."

* "My parents do so much for me I feel pressure to do well, and when I don't I feel guilty."

* "There's a lot I can't tell them because I know they will get mad."

When these are the thoughts on the juniors' minds they cannot possibly focus on each shot and play their best. This book will give you alternatives to the non-productive parenting behaviors that result in comment like the above.

♛

## Parenting that produces champions

*"Treat your child as you would the person you would like him to become, and he will become that person."*
– Dr. Haim Ginott, noted psychologist

At the age of 15 Mina Harigae won the 2004 California Women's Amateur Championship, playing against women who played tournament golf long before Mina was born. That may not seem an unusual accomplishment in this day of talented juniors, however in this case, it was Mina's fourth consecutive state amateur victory!

Mina was a young swimmer who enjoyed going to the golf course to spend time with her father. As an 8-year-old she decided she would rather play golf than swim. Her parents took her to a junior clinic sponsored by the Salvation Army. Soon she got involved in junior programs on the Monterey Peninsula. Mina showed extraordinary talent and motivation. At age of 12 she won the first in her string of California State Amateurs. She said her goal is to dominate girl's junior golf (as of this writing she is ranked number 6 on the Golfweek/Titleist Ranking), to earn a college golf scholarship and then play on the pro tour.

The Harigaes are less involved in Mina's golf than the average golfing parents; they are too busy running their restaurant. Their values and actions have taught Mina what is important in life. "It doesn't matter to my parents if I play golf or not," Mina said. "School is the most important thing to them. My parents always support and encourage me, they never criticize – unless I start to get a big head. They teach me to stay humble."

I asked Mina what kind of advice she has for parents of golfing juniors. "So many parents try to force their kids to practice or criticize them all the time," she said. "I'd tell them, **"Give your kids space, lighten up, encourage them. Stop criticizing and let them do their thing.""**

♚

Jaime Diaz, a former college golfer who has been a golf writer for about 25 years, was very close to Tiger Woods' family and observed their interaction during junior tournaments. When Tiger didn't play well, there was never any recrimination from his parents. "They kind of shrugged it off," he said. That's because Tiger was playing for himself, not for his parents. Diaz said that when he saw juniors reprimanded and criticized after playing, he could "see the life and joy go out of a kid."

"Fun is the most important element for a junior to continue improving," Diaz said. "If he's having fun he will improve. If he is grinding, he won't improve."

♛

Some parents just seem to know the right way to imspire and get the best from their kids. Perhaps it's a holdover from their experiences growing up, or the result of education. That's not to say they don't make mistakes, everyone does. However, their children respect the parents and their decisions and respond positively in competition, both in golf and in academics.

I met Aree Song, her twin sister Naree and their father In Jong in 2000, at the first LPGA major of the year, the Kraft Nabisco Championship. The summer before, Aree's victory in the U.S. Girls Junior Championship at age 12 made her the youngest USGA champion in history. At age 13, the twins had a special exemption to play in the Kraft Nabisco Championship – and Aree made it into the final group for Sunday, finishing 10th. By age 17, Aree received a special exemption to play the LPGA Tour in 2004 after earning her place at the tour qualifying school finals. Naree joined her sister on the LPGA Tour during the 2005 season.

During our discussions, Aree said, "We were raised to have fun with golf and keep it simple. Technique was not emphasized too early. We explored our own potential with the right pro for us. We love playing and practicing. When we have disagreements with our parents they are always settled on a good note so we can perform the next day. Our father has never yelled at us or punished us if we didn't play up to his expectations."

Aree also said there definitely is discipline in the home. The children were taught to respect their elders. Education and healthy habits are stressed, and standards are high, yet the children were encouraged to have fun and be happy in what they do. When I asked how they felt about their parents' presence at tournaments, Aree said, "When they are there, I feel peace of mind."

♔

Stacy Prammanasudh qualified for the 2004 Kraft Nabisco Championship by virtue of being 10th on the LPGA Tour money list. She was named 2003 Futures Tour Player of the Year, finishing first on that money list to earn exempt status on the LPGA Tour for 2004. Stacy was not groomed as a child for a professional golf career. She decided to turn professional only after a successful college career at the University of Tulsa. She was three-time Academic all-American and first-team all-American from 1999 to 2002. Stacy told me she decided to turn professional because, "I felt I owed it to myself to see how far I could take it. I didn't want to look back someday and wonder if I could have made it."

Stacy's father was her only teacher and he made golf fun. He taught her the basics and she worked and experimented with a swing that took her to a No. 2 national ranking during her senior year in college. She was never forced to practice, never criticized. The values stressed in her home were education, respect for elders and to do whatever you decide to do 110 percent.

Corrina: Rees is a junior champion with designs on the LPGA Tour. For three years, she has been the only girl on the varsity high school team (there are not enough girl golfers at her school to form a team.) She has a number of trophies. "I have awesome parents," Corinna said. "My parents are both coaches, so they know how to get the best out of me. My dad is a great golfer, but even though he knows the game, he doesn't correct my swing or bombard me with advice. My folks ask me if I am open to their coaching and suggestions. If I am, they coach me. If I'm not ready to listen or learn, they back off. They are always positive. They always point out what I am doing well. After a tournament, instead of telling me what I did wrong, we talk about what I need to improve – but we only do it when I am ready to discuss it. They let me cool down first."

When 15 year-old Matthew Garcia called to tell me he had broken through and shot 69 at a Future Collegiate World Tour Tournament, he talked about his relationship with his father and mother. "I wouldn't be where I am if it weren't for my parents. We're not rich and they don't know much about golf, but they give me every opportunity they can. They don't criticize my playing, or tell me what I should have done when I make mistakes. A lot of the other kids' fathers yell at them, telling them what they did wrong and what to do. I'm glad my parents let me work things out myself and with my coach. It's making me more mentally mature."

Additional junior golfers interviewed for this book offered positive comments about their parents:

- ✦ "My mom / dad / parents will do anything to help me."

- ✦ "They tell me that if I decide not to compete, they will support anything I decide to do – but I have to do something."

- ✦ "It doesn't matter how I play. I know they love me."

- ✦ "If I'm playing poorly, they tell me everyone has days like that and I have another chance to play tomorrow."

- ✦ "After a round we always go out for something to eat, and have some fun together."

Scott Rude, son of nationally renowned golf writer Jeff Rude, said he is very grateful he has the parents he has. "Every decision they made was what was best for me, not necessarily my golf game. My mom was my cheerleader. She taught me about love and family, compassion, integrity, and to be of service. My dad taught me a good work ethic, no excuses, discipline. He was very supportive and loving. In spite of all these positive influences, I found that when my dad gave me advice about my golf, I gritted my teeth. Someone else could tell me the same thing and I would accept it, but I resisted advice from my dad."

I assured Scott that his response was a normal for a young man who was becoming his own person and preparing for independence and the real world. This is an important point for those of you who are noticing that your junior has suddenly changed from an "agreeable, compliant child" to a "resistant adolescent."

♛

# ACTION IDEA
## A Questionnaire for Parents:

*How do you compare to the parents described above?*
*Answer each of the following questions thoughtfully and honestly.*
*Assign a number – 1. never, 2. sometimes, 3. about half the time,*
*4. usually, 5. always*

\_\_\_\_ 1. My child knows that the most important thing is to excel at golf and to win.

\_\_\_\_ 2. I know how difficult golf is and am very under standing when it comes to the pressure of competition.

\_\_\_\_ 3. I let my child know that I am spending a lot of time and money on her and it is her responsibility to make the best use of her opportunities.

\_\_\_\_ 4. I am happy when my child plays her best, even though she might shoot one of the higher scores.

\_\_\_\_ 5. When my child plays poorly I am embarrassed and wonder what the other parents think.

\_\_\_\_ 6. Playing golf and competing was my child's idea.

\_\_\_\_ 7. It has always been my dream to be a professional golfer, but I never had the opportunity.

\_\_\_\_ 8. When I am walking the course with my child and he looks at me, he sees a happy proud parent.

\_\_\_\_ 9. I know I show disapproval when my child hits a poor shot, but I get so frustrated that I can't help it.

_____ 10. As long as my child loves playing and competing I am happy. The outcome of the tournament is not the important thing to me.

_____ 11. When my child makes the same mistakes over and over, I get very upset.

_____ 12. I encourage my child to have interests other than golf.

_____ 13. I do have a tendency to get loud and critical when I am angry.

_____ 14. My child knows by my behavior that I love her no matter what she chooses to do with her life.

_____ 15. I am tired of the way my child takes his opportunities for granted.

_____ 16. I actively use golf as a way to teach my child about values and life in general.

_____ 17. I try to correct my child's errors at the earliest possible time. It's important that she knows what she did wrong so she can correct it right away.

_____ 18. Everyone in our family knows who are the parents and who are the children.

_____ 19. I need to constantly monitor my child because he does so many "stupid" or irresponsible things.

_____ 20. I listen to my child respectfully and consider his opinions.

_____ 21. My child often tells me I am not fair, or don't understand him.

_____ 22. My child has a sense of true appreciation for his privileges.

_____ 23. It is important to me that my child takes golf seriously, practices hard and knows that the purpose of competing is to win.

_____ 24. If my child my never gets a college scholarship nor makes it to the tour, that's fine with me. I just want him to develop character and be happy in what he does.

_____ 25. I am having trouble getting my child to practice.

_____ 26. I trust my child to be responsible and make good (age appropriate) decisions.

_____ 27. I tend to be fairly impatient and critical but that's O.K., because I look for results.

_____ 28. It's hard to get my child off the golf course (or practice range).

_____ 29. My child is moody much of the time.

_____ 30. I am my child's greatest cheerleader.

*Now for the scoring system: Each question has a maximum of 5 points. Add up your score on the odd numbers (the maximum score is 75). Add up your score on the even numbers (again, the maximum score is 75). Your goal is to go low on the odd numbered statements, and high on the even. Since this rating is totally subjective, the only guideline is that the even score should be considerably higher than the odd total. As you read this book, you will get a good understanding of each question and how it impacts your champion. Ask your child to rate you. This could make for a very enlightening discussion.*

♛

# PART II:
## THE BUILDING BLOCKS
## OF CHAMPIONS

### THREE BASIC PRINCIPLES

You will build a champion if you use three basic principles as your foundation.

1. Love your child unconditionally.
2. Support your child in achieving his dreams.
3. Teach your child how to live responsibly.

If your actions are consistent with these principles you will be a champion parent. These principles must be practiced in a balanced way. This book is your guide to balance.

*"Any virtue carried to an extreme becomes a vice."*

Unconditional love without teaching can raise a spoiled, unruly child who becomes a self-absorbed adult. Teaching without love often raises a competent but resentful or emotionally disabled adult. Support without teaching produces an incapacitated or incompetent adult, while support without love can lead to a cynical or emotionally deprived adult. Love without support can have several outcomes – one outcome might be an underachieving adult who hasn't fulfilled his potential, or in the best case, it could result in a self-reliant, creative super-producer and extraordinary champion.

# PRINCIPLE # 1:
# LOVE YOUR CHILD UNCONDITIONALLY

*"The best way to appreciate your children is to imagine yourself without them."*

You have been given a most precious gift. The gift of a life to cherish and influence. When your child is born you are in awe of the miracle and vow to love and protect her forever. The act of birth is the first moment of separation. Your child is a separate being who, though a part of you, is different from you. This child was born with gifts, talents, a personality, needs and desires that are separate from yours. On the other hand your child is really just like you. She can feel pain, comfort, security, hunger, cold, and frustration. As she grows she will have both positive emotions such as joy and excitement, and negative emotions, including fears, anxieties doubts – all the feelings you have. As you raise your child, you must always be aware that you are the child's world, and you have the power to cause both joy and pain. When you do cause pain, ask yourself if that was your intent? If it was your intent, ask yourself if you could teach the same lesson in a less painful way. And then seriously consider why you would even want to cause harm to your most precious gift.

♕

*"I desire that there be as many different persons in the world as possible. I would have each one be careful to find out and preserve his own way."*
 – Henry David Thoreau

**To love your child is to recognize his uniqueness and wholeheartedly accept him for who he is, not lamenting that he doesn't fit your image. It is to uncover your child's**

**gifts and nurture his interests.**

When you love your child unconditionally, you let go of what you want your child to become and help your child fully explore and develop his gifts. It may be golf, it may be another sport, or it may be art, music or computers. Love the child who chooses not follow in your footsteps. Love the child who does follow in your footsteps, but doesn't measure up to your level of success. Linda Miller, wife of Hall of Fame golf champion Johnny Miller, said it is interesting that none of their sons who chose a professional golf career have done as well, competitively, as their father. However, they have found success. For example, John Miller Jr., the eldest son, discovered his gift in golf is teaching. Without exception, the six Miller children are all loved unconditionally for who they are as individuals.

♛

My son Seth created mischief at school from the time he started kindergarten until he dropped out of college. He was a ranked junior tennis player between the ages of 8 and 12. The pro at our tennis club told me he was a shoe-in for a college tennis scholarship if he would only practice. A scholarship was appealing, since Seth was my third child and I was a single mother at the time. However, his interests expanded to photography, art, and surfing. He did play on his high school tennis team, but was not willing to take his game to higher levels. As a child he was loved for his energy, creativity his leadership and goal setting determination. At home he was taught respect, accountability and high moral standards. His mediocre grades and mischievous behavior were tolerated as integral parts of a creative personality that ultimately found full expression in the adult world. By the time he turned 30 my college dropout son had created a multimillion-dollar business, and then developed a passion for golf. He approached golf with the same zeal that he approached cartooning as a 10 year-old and surfing as a teenager. It took him only 2 years to become a 6-handicap and play in the Pro-Am in Tiger Woods' Target World Challenge (I never could share his interest in skateboards and surfing, but now we do share golf!)

♔

**One of the most serious errors parents make is to treat their child as though he has no feelings. To love your child is to recognize him as a human being with feelings.**

Linda Miller shepherded the Miller boys through junior golf. "I don't understand parents who berate their children for making mistakes on the course," she said. "Don't they know that the child is out there trying his best? Golf is such a complex and difficult game; there are so many things that can influence a score." Given the pressure inherent in the competitive model, as well as the emotional battering some kids receive, the Millers' son, Todd, suggested that competitive junior golf not start before age 16.

I, too, wonder at parents who embarrass or berate their children in public. If you were berated or embarrassed in front of the people you work for or with, or in front of your friends, would you react with, "Oh I better change my behavior," or would you dig in, rationalize, and be resentful? I'm sure it would be the latter.

While conducting interviews for this book I heard many stories that made me wonder what some parents are thinking. The father of a current tour player slapped his daughter in public at a junior tournament. Another father was so angry with his daughter's play that he drove off and told her to find her own way home from the course. Defending her title in a junior world championship, one young girl lost a playoff after her father had her up against a wall, yelling and berating her for missing the putt that forced the playoff. Her opponent said, "I knew the championship was mine. Her father upset her so much that she was shaking."

♛

When I suggest to some parents that they really are putting too much pressure on their children, they say things like, "I want so badly for her to do well, it's what she wants too." It's true, the child does want to play well and win. But does she want to win for herself or does she want to win to earn your love? When you criticize her course management, second-guess her shots and point out all her errors, you only will generate resentment and resistance. There are better ways to respond. Instead of saying that her putting stinks and demand she practice her putting for three hours a day – which she would perceive as punishment – ask her how you can support her: "How can I help you achieve your goals? What can I do to help you play as well as you are capable?

After his son finished a winter afternoon session with me, a father wanted his son to go outside and practice putting and chipping till dark. I knew the junior had spent six hours on the range before his appointment with me, so I suggested to the father that his junior sit quietly indoors and review mental techniques. "Oh, 'Thank You Dr. Bee," said the junior, with a look of tremendous relief. "It's so cold outside."

**A question to keep in your mind at all times: "If I was being treated the way I am treating my child, how would I feel?"**

♛

**Another question to ask yourself, "Would I treat an acquain-**

tance or another child the way I am treating my child?"

I was on the range at a 2003 U.S. Junior Girls qualifier. I heard a father yelling at his daughter. The child, who looked like she was about 12, hit a few more balls while the father continued his tirade. Her shot-making deteriorated. Suddenly the father grabbed the club at the top of the back swing and roughly "helped" his daughter swing. "Do it that way!" he shouted. The girl was in tears and the father turned and stormed off in anger.

A few minutes later, the father was talking to another young competitor smiling. I moved closer to try to over-hear the conversation. This time the father was smiling, as he patiently demonstrated a backswing for this child. She reproduced it. And he then patted her shoulder gently and turned to have a conversation with her father.

Isn't it ironic that the father treated another child whom he may never see again with more kindness, patience and respect than he gave his own daughter? Parents say that they love their children, yet their behavior often suggests the opposite. Why is it necessary to yell at, strike, insult, or cause emotional pain to someone you love? What would happen if everyone treated their loved ones with the same consideration respect and patience that they afford to strangers? I suggest you try it.

*"Treat your loved ones like strangers"*
– Dr. Bee

♕

A difficult question to ask – and answer truthfully – is, "Do I love my child unconditionally for who he is, or do I love him for being an extension of me and for what he does that makes me proud?" You probably would answer, "Of course I love my child." If you have more than one child, you would also say that you love them all equally. But research indicates that this is not true necessarily true.

Laura (not her real name) was a talented young golfer, but not as talented as her brother. Their father claimed to love both his children equally; his actions suggested otherwise. Laura felt unloved. She decided to work harder and harder on her game, and in school, thinking lower scores and higher grades would win in her father's love. She did get some recognition for her efforts, but not nearly as much as her favored brother. Eventually, the strain of competing for the love of an insensitive father led to a serious emotional breakdown.

Never say to your child, "Why can't you be more like your brother?" or compare her unfavorably to her peers: "If you would work as hard as Hannah does you'd get better grades." "If you would practice as much as your brother, you'd win once in a while too." And for goodness sake let go of the, "You don't know how lucky you are, I would have given anything to have the opportunities you have."

It's acceptable to share incidents from your childhood with your children in discussions of family history, or tell amusing, inspiring, or even painful stories. But this must never be done critically, or in a context that suggests your child isn't good enough, or unappreciative.

♕

**To love your child unconditionally is to be grateful that he is healthy and able to play golf, instead of being upset that he finished only 20th at his last tournament.**

# ACTION IDEA

Some years ago, a friend, the father of three teenage children, died unexpectedly of a heart attack at age 47. Immediately, my thoughts went back to comments he had made recently at a wedding. "Jim is going to play number two on the high school golf team. I'm going to have fun watching him play. ... This is such a beautiful occasion, I'm looking forward to the time I can walk Allison down the aisle." Now six months later, I was at his funeral telling a friend about our last conversation. "It's a tragedy to go so young," I said. "At least their 'I love yous' were up to date," replied my friend. She went on, "That family made a point of telling each other they loved one other, so when Jim Sr. died, there was no unfinished business and no regrets over what was said in anger. This family's last memories are loving ones."

I thought about "normal" conditions in my household. Sometimes my kids went off to school with my angry words in their heads. If I were to go down in a plane on a business trip, I would not want my children's last memory of me to be something unkind that came out of my mouth in a moment of anger. And if one of my children died in an auto accident, I could not live with the thought that they left this world feeling my negativity. At that funeral, my life changed. From that day on, every conversation with my children begins and ends in kind and loving words.

Through the years I have shared that story with thousands of people in my lectures. Many have contacted me to tell me what a difference a simple message has made in their relationships and lives.

*Keep your "I love yous" up to date.*

# PRINCIPLE #2:
## SUPPORT YOUR CHILD'S DREAM

*"Open as many doors as possible, but don't push them through."*
– Matt Kuchar, 1997 U.S. Amateur
Champion and Professional Golfer

I remember the huge smile on Matt's face as he sank his putt on 18 to finish 14th in the 1998 U.S. Open at The Olympic Club in San Francisco. I also remember his father's exuberance throughout the tournament – problematic to some pros since Dad caddied for Matt. When I talked to Matt about his introduction to golf, he told me that he had started out playing tennis with his father, a competitive tennis player. Then when he was about 12, Matt and his father took up golf together. Matt fell in love with the game and never had to be encouraged to practice or play. He was self-motivated.

He learned passion for the game and for competition from his father. And from his mother he learned manners and how to behave. The three made a winning team. When I asked how his father responded when he played poorly, Matt said, "When I was on the top of my game, or when my game was off, my father was always proud and supportive, no matter what." With that kind of support a golfer is free to play his game, experiment and learn from mistakes without periodic poor play eroding his sense of self-worth.

♔

When Bill Haas, son of Jay Haas, missed getting his 2005 PGA Tour card and exempt playing privileges by only two strokes at Qualifying School, he was very disappointed. It was his dream to be half of a father-son team on the "big" tour. He had been the 2003-2004 college player of the year at Wake Forest. In 2004 he played in nine PGA Tour events on exemptions, earning more than $300,000. In spite of the disappointment of failing short of his expectations, he said "I know my father will be very supportive." Earlier, his father had told me that the secret to raising champions was to love and support them – no matter what. Luckily, Bill wasn't going to face the criticism and Monday morning quarterbacking that so many other players get from their less supportive parents. Jaime Diaz, who has written about father-son combinations, said that Jay stays in the background and lets Bill find his way and become his own person, rather than a reflection of the father.

♛

Paula Creamer's parents are the epitome of supportive parents. When I originally connected with the Creamers, Paula was 17 and the No. 1-ranked girls junior in the country. During the 2004 season Paula played in seven LPGA Tour tournaments, making the cut in all of them – finishing second in the Shop-Rite Classic and tied for 13th in the U.S. Women's Open. Still in high school, she was medalist at the LPGA Tour Qualifying School, achieving one of her goals: to play on the LPGA Tour. I asked her father, Paul Creamer, "If your daughter decided to give up golf, would you love her anyway?" His look suggested that was a really stupid question as he answered, "Of course I'd still love and support her. I only want her to be happy." The Creamers changed their lives to accommodate their daughter's dream by moving to Florida to be near Paula while she attended the Leadbetter Academy. Paul could have said that after all the sacrifices the family made, and the time and money put into Paula's golf, they would be really angry if she gave it all up. But he didn't. It is obvious when I speak to and observe the Creamers, that their love and support is pure and unconditional. This is a champion family.

"Support" does not mean buying your child the latest equipment, cutest clothes, arrange for lessons with the "best" professional. That's OK as long as you can afford it without depriving the rest of the family. **But the child must also have a sense of appreciation and exchange – that's how life works. If nothing is required of the child, she could turn out to be a spoiled unpleasant person.**

A parent recently complained about his daughter, who was now in her mid-20s and totally irresponsible. Though her golf was good enough to earn a college scholarship she dropped out of school after one semester. She can't keep a job for more than a few months, runs up bills, and is now costing the parents more than when she was in private school and they were traveling to tournaments. I reminded the father that when she was growing up she could depend on her parents to treat her like a princess, to do everything for her and clean up all her mistakes. She never learned to be responsible for her actions. Instead she developed a sense of entitlement that could ruin her life.

"Support" does not mean "support everything she does and give her whatever it takes to make her happy." It means support the activities she is committed to and is willing to put time and energy into. Children need to experiment with a variety of activities. You may find your child committed to soccer for awhile, gymnastics or music for awhile, and golf for awhile. Let her explore and learn, give her opportunities, drive her to activities and provide some professional training or lessons. But if this is not the right activity for your child, support her in finding something to be excited about and committed to.

**Support means to be a rock, a base on which your children can stand. It doesn't mean pulling them up from above.**

Stacy Prammanasudh comes from a working-class family. There was no money for college. When Stacy showed exceptional motivation and talent for golf at age 14, it was the first time anyone thought it might be a way to ensure a college education. Stacy's dad supported all her efforts and spent weekends walking tournaments with his daughter. When friends questioned the amount of time he was investing in her he said, "It is my privilege to walk with my daughter". He never criticized, he never pushed; he just encouraged. Now as a professional on the LPGA Tour, Stacy likes having Dad on her bag. "He is my comfort factor," she said.

♛

Eddie Merrins, the famed "Little Pro" at the Bel-Air Country Club in Los Angeles and former UCLA golf coach, talked to me about his junior experience. He was exposed to golf by his friends when he was 11. His parents did not play, but since Eddie was hooked and spent most of the daylight hours at the local golf club, his parents joined to give him a place to play and practice. The adult golfing members of the club "adopted" and mentored him. By age 14, he was involved in the club competitions. His parents encouraged his golf and gave him every opportunity to play. In addition they made sure he took school seriously. Support is providing what one can so a child committed to an activity can achieve his potential.

♛

Sometimes support is mainly verbal. This is often the most appreciated kind of support. Ben Salk, a promising 13-

year-old junior who counts golf as one of his passions, said, "My parents are very supportive. They don't try to control me. They give me tips and make suggestions. They don't criticize bad shots, but give me good feedback. They are very positive and keep my spirits and confidence high so I can play my best."

I asked my grown children about their recollections of their junior tennis – and other aspects of their childhood. My son Seth and younger daughter Nicole, said the most important recollections they have is of being told that they could do anything they decided to do. And, Seth added, "I remember being told that whatever I chose to do, I would do well."

They both loved playing tennis. Since we had money only for essentials, my support was mostly verbal. Seth said he had happy memories of earning spending money by stringing racquets at the tennis club, beginning at age 9. (He wasn't quite so fond of hosing down courts.) And even though he had been a ranked junior player for four years when he decided to stop competing at age 12, there were no repercussions. He said he discovered there were other things he wanted to experience. Throughout his life, whenever he decided to commit to something, he has done exceptionally well. His championship life is not the result of large financial and time investments on the part of his parents, it is the result of the high self-esteem developed from verbal support.

♔

## Whose life is this anyway?

**Support your child in living his dream. Do not expect your child to fulfill your dreams.**

Dr. Ian Tofler was the chair of the Sport Psychiatry Committee of the American Academy of Child and Adolescent Psychiatry when he coauthored *"Keeping Your Kids Out Front Without Kicking Them From Behind."* He developed and researched a concept called Achievement by Proxy ( ABP). He says:

> *"In a healthy "by proxy" experience, a supportive parent or adult can vicariously experience a child's success or failure and at the same time realize that the child is a separate individual with her own unique needs and goals. In supportive ABP situations, financial and social benefits from a child's success are not the parent's primary goal. These collateral benefits are no more than a pleasant side effect. The child or adolescent's individuality is acknowledged, and the involved adults have the ability to distinguish the child's needs and goals from their own. ABP is normal, healthy, and sane."* (page 15)

Dr. Tofler goes on to say that in some cases parents cross the line from supportive parenting to abnormal distorted parenting behavior. This he labels Achievement by Proxy Distortion (ABPD).

The Michele Wie phenomenon can be seen as an example of ABPD. Her family put her in situations inappropriate for a child and sought recognition from the press. The media hype is out of proportion to her actual achievements, considering her lack of spectacular performance as a junior. Michelle has tremendous talent, but is being exploited shamelessly. As a young teen she is much too young to be playing in professional tournaments with men. She also has far too many women's professional tournaments on her schedule for a child her age. The pressure is enormous and cannot be beneficial to her mental and emotional health. B.J. Wie is quoted in Ron Sirak's *GolfWorld* article ("The Parent Trap," Feb. 20, 2004): "I want to do everything

I can to increase her Q rating. I am a very calculating person. Everyone wins when my daughter plays. The charities sell more tickets, the tour gets more exposure, and Michelle gets better known." He failed to say, "Dad wins too," since the minute she turns pro she will have millions of dollars in endorsements and Dad will get some of his huge financial investment back. Michelle's best interests seem to be very low on the priority list. Note that B.J. points out that, "Michelle gets better known." That can backfire as her performance comes under more scrutiny. If she fails to achieve her goals, or her performance disappoints the public, she can suffer serious psychological harm. Dr. Tofler:

> "An adult is exhibiting ABPD when the external benefits of the child's achievements become important, concurrent, or even primary goals for the adult, not a simple dividend of success. The potential benefits to the parents of a high-achieving child include the potential for fame, financial gain, career advancement, and social recognition and respect. When an adult puts the attainment of these benefits before the needs and goals of the child, he or she becomes capable of a unique form of child abuse and neglect." (page 19)

♛

Many parents have unrealistic expectations for their kids and push them to turn pro prematurely. The junior usually is a local golf star and may have a couple of wins on the junior or amateur circuit – and is immediately seen as being ready for the tour. The glamour and money of professional golf seduces players and parents into trying to compete at the highest levels before the player has the emotional maturity and mental stamina to succeed. Jay Coffin, who writes for *Golfweek* magazine and specializes in junior golf and college golf, told me that one parent made the comment that in retrospect, he regrets pushing his child to cut college short, turn pro and go to the tour qualifying school. Not measuring up can erode confidence in a young and relatively inexperienced competitor. Coffin suggests, and I agree, that a young player should have several years experience beating everyone in his age group before having expectations of doing well on tour. **A supportive parent makes sure his child's emotional and mental development are in line with his physical skills before presenting the player to the world.**

The same principle holds true for your younger child. Do not push her into serious competition before she is emotionally mature enough to learn and benefit from her experiences.

♚

## Create a nurturing environment

**Your child comes into the world with potential. The environment will determine if that child's potential is realized, or whether that potential is undermined. You, the parent, are in charge of that environment.**

Though a seed has potential, the soil in which it is planted, the amount of sunshine, water and fertilizer it gets will determine the hardiness of the plant. Orchids are beautiful plants that can bloom again and again when they are grown in the environment that provides them proper nourishment. Roses and geraniums won't survive in the orchid environment. Each plant has special requirements.

Plants are fairly simple. Get directions for the right combination of water, nutrients, light, follow the directions, and your results will be predictable. Children, on the other hand, are complex beings whose physical, emotional and spiritual needs must be addressed if they are to grow into champion children, and later into champion adults.

Your job as a supportive parent is to provide an environment in which the needs of your developing child are addressed. This is the hardest, most time-consuming, most frustrating yet rewarding job on the planet.

+ You must provide a safe haven for the child so that whenever he is troubled, or even in trouble, he has a place in which he feels safe. The ideal situation would be that your child feels safe enough to tell you the truth about anything and everything. Kids lie because they believe, "If my parents found out they would kill me!"

+ A nurturing home environment is one in which there is minimal turmoil and arguments, where parents are in accord on important issues, especially child rearing

+ Structure and order and a reliable routine are important. Children need the security of predictability.

+ Your child requires proper nutrition, so you must provide the foods that have the nutrients needed for health and growth. This one small part of parenting is a major issue in many families and has led to the crisis of overweight American children.

+ You must provide the child with opportunities for self-sufficiency so that he can always take care of himself and then be the parent in his own household someday.

+ You must see to it that the child is educated in the things he needs to know in order to grow into a functioning adult. This involves formal schooling and informal education in life skills. (More in the next section.)

✦ It is not necessary that you provide your child with all the material things he wants. An Ipod, the newest putter and a set of wheels at 16 are nice, but not essential. All parents want to provide the best for their children – but the real "best" is time, love, support and values.

# ACTION IDEA

## A Support Agreement
*(This action idea is a spin-off of the Peter Drucker example. It is not for 6 year-olds; it begins to work around age 10 or 11.)*

✦ Set aside a time to talk to your child and ask him, "What do I do that makes you feel supported? What other things could I do that makes you feel supported?" It's important that you both agree on what support means.

✦ Take one or two of his suggestions and promise to do that. For example, if he says, "When I'm ready to tee off give me an encouraging sign." Make it a point to remember that and follow through. Sometimes it will be something you should stop doing. "Don't shake your head and walk away when I'm not playing well."

✦ Now you can tell your child how he can support you. "Make sure you are ready to go – clubs in the car, sweaters, snacks, etc. when it's time to leave for the course. Say thank you for driving, or thank you for walking with me, etc., when I do things for you."

**Write a simple agreement.**

## SAMPLE AGREEMENT

It is our intent to have a loving supportive parent-child relationship. To accomplish this, I, _____
(parent's name)

promise to _____

_____

_____

_____

I, _____ promise to
(child's name)

_____

_____

_____

_____

If either party fails to live up to this agreement, we will calmly discuss the problem and if necessary, will arbitrate with a neutral third party.

_____     _____
Signed                                   Date
          ( Parent)

_____     _____
Signed                                   Date
          (Child)

# PRINCIPLE #3:
# TEACH YOUR CHILD TO LIVE RESPONSIBLY

*"Well done is better than well said."*
– Ben Franklin

**"Walk your Talk."** Your child will learn far more from observing your actions than any lessons you try to teach him with words.

Questions to ask yourself frequently are:

✦ " What does my child need to know to live the kind of life I want for him?"

✦ " What kind of a role model or example am I?"

✦ " Do I want my child's behavior to reflect mine?" (It will, you know, whether you want it to or not.)

The father of one of my junior clients often complained about his son's lack of focus and patience. The son and I have been working on that. Finally, after three months of complaining, the father said, "I kind of understand that. I'm like that myself." In order for the son to change, the father must change first and set the example. He cannot expect more from his son than he does from himself.

A highly visible junior golfer was known for his disrespectful behavior and foul language. People who know the family told me his father is like that, too. It seems the young man's grandfather also was a golfer with a temperament unbecoming a gentleman – and golf is a "gentleman's game." Three generations of males in that family have a reputation for rude behavior, so whatever the sons might have been told about appropriate behavior was discounted. They learned by imitation.

A caddy told me the player whose bag he used to carry is selfish and mean spirited. "His brother and mother are like that too," he said.

*You create the footsteps your child will follow in.*

♛

Golf is a game of integrity. If your behavior as a parent does not reflect integrity, your child will do what you do, not what you say. I vividly remember an event that shook my trust. My father, a strict man, taught me to always tell the truth. As a matter fact, he added scare tactics. He modified the Pinocchio story – you remember, Pinocchio's nose grew whenever he lied. My father's version was that a lie would cause my ears to grow as large as Mickey Mouse's. That threat carried a lot of weight with me when I was 4 or 5. As a result, when I was a small child I was always fearfully truthful. When I was about 10, I was in my father's furniture store when he was selling a chair to a customer. He told her the chair was the latest style and the highest quality for a bargain price – and since someone else looked at it earlier, if she went home to think about it, it probably would be gone when she returned. Later that evening, I overheard him telling my mother he finally got rid of that ugly old chair that had been sitting around in the store forever. As an adult, I see salesmanship in my father's lie, but as a child my trust was shaken when I experienced my father doing what he taught me never to do. I also remember being confused about what was appropriate behavior.

✦ You cannot teach truthfulness unless you are truthful.

✦ If you blow up when your child makes what you consider a "foolish" mistake on the course, you are teaching him to blow up. How can you teach your kids to keep their cool under pressure if you can't keep yours?

✦ You cannot expect your kids to respect others if they hear you make derogatory comments.

✦ You cannot teach your children to be punctual if you are constantly late and can't be counted on to be where you say you will be.

✦ You cannot teach your kids to avoid drugs or alcohol if they see you consistently using alcohol as a stress reducer.

✦ You cannot teach your child respect for the course if he sees you flick cigarette or cigar butts into the rough.

✦ You cannot teach your child respect for the law if you break it in many "little" ways – i.e. speeding when you think there are no police around, trying to fix traffic tickets, or driving after several drinks.

♔

**If you want to raise a champion child, look at yourself first.** As you read this section, ask yourself if there might be a little touch-up work you want to do on yourself to acquire the characteristics you want to see in your child. This book makes many suggestions, sometimes by telling you to ask yourself questions – and also suggesting that you ask your family for input. Pay attention to what you discover.

♔

# Teach your child values

Johnny and Linda Miller's son Todd withdrew from the Sunday final of the 2004 Utah State Amateur. He said he did not want to play on the Sabbath. Todd would rather give up the championship than go against his religious beliefs. His beliefs preclude a professional career, but he has made what for him is a value-based choice. Not all members of Todd's family feel so strongly about working on the Sabbath, but they respect and support his decision. Is dedication to your faith something that you want to strengthen? It may not be to keep the Sabbath with as much rigor as Todd Miller, but perhaps you want to take a closer look at the Golden Rule, or the Ten Commandments.

The Miller family is steeped in integrity. Andy Miller called a penalty on himself at the tour qualifying school that resulted in his failing to move to the next phase – precluding a tour card for another year. It is not unusual to find that a tour player calls a penalty on himself giving up a lot of money. What goes on in your family? Is the emphasis on score and winning so strong that your child would be tempted to cheat? One junior told me she was aware that a parent changed a scorecard for his child. That parent, and eventually the child, are not to be trusted. Golf is a reflection of life.

♛

"Dad, should I turn professional?" asked Stacy Prammanasudh during her senior year at the University of Tulsa. "That's up to you," he said. "When you have graduated from college, you have fulfilled your responsibility to your family. Now the rest of your life is for you."

Many parents have education as the highest priority. Jon McLean told me that in his family, school is more important than golf. Jon's dad, Jim Mclean, is one of the best teaching professionals in America. Jim founded the Future Collegiate World Tour – one of the premier golf tours for juniors – yet in his home, education was given the highest priority.

Jon and his brother Matt also were taught the value of hard work: "Always try your hardest. Hard work pays off." Chris Riley, member of the PGA Tour and 2004 U.S. Ryder Cup Team, said his father demonstrated the value of hard work with his actions. 13-year-old Ben Salk said, "My parents told me that if I want to improve, it takes work." And at the same age, when junior Christina Stockton decided to play tournaments, she was also told golf would now take consistent practice and work. It's almost a given that work is a value taught by parents with high aspirations for their children. How does your child perceive work? Is it as an unwelcome chore, or does he perceive work as something that will help him achieve his goals? Do you demonstrate hard work, as Chris Riley's father did? Can you make "working" at golf fun? That's ideal.

♛

In our society there is a very strong work ethic. However, sometimes we go overboard. "All work and no play makes Jack a dull boy," is an old cliche, but it is borne out by new research that suggests that people have to "play" in order to remain mentally healthy. Anything that a person thoroughly enjoys can be considered play. Whatever results in positive emotions and provides a relief from concerns, the pressure to perform, or the necessity to make a living is considered play. All of the champion performers I spoke to said that their parents emphasized that golf was fun. "It was always fun," said Aree Song. "I was always having fun," said Chris Riley. Paul Creamer insisted that his daughter Paula's teaching pro make lessons fun.

Professional Jolene Stockton said her teacher, Johnny Miller's father, Larry Miller, made it fun. And Phil Mickelson wanted to play junior golf as long has he could because it was so much fun.

Championship golf takes a balance of work and fun. Are you making your child's practice a grind? Is your supervision and insistence on perfectionism detracting from the joy of experimentation and discovery and the exhilaration of well-played shots? If you are too serious, put some more fun and games into your junior's life. As Mina Harigae said, "Lighten up."

*Tired happens when fun doesn't*
— Unnamed 5 year-old

♛

Is the importance of family one of your values? Family as a value is given a great deal of lip service. Ask yourself if you are primarily concerned about the welfare of your family, or if you are demonstrating the greater importance of tournament victories. Perhaps you are even living your dream through your child. So many tour players are at odds with their parents because of too much pressure and criticism, and lack of unconditional love. I have already discussed the O'Hairs, but there are many more. In 2004, Golfweek Magazine's Ron Sirak wrote about the conflict between LPGA Tour champion Rachel Hetherington and her father. She won eight times on tour during an 11-year separation between them. Jeff Rude's article in Golfweek detailed the rift between PGA Tour member Briney Baird and his father, who both are quoted as calling themselves stubborn. They are demonstrating "being right" as a value. Are you considering the impact of golf on your family as a whole, and on your relationship with your child?

Each family has it's own set of values. As a family, examine those values and the reasons behind them – and more important, live those values.

♛

## Teach your child about character traits that are important to you and your family

**Persistence, desire for excellence, ambition and humility are a few of the traits that champions exhibit.**

My interview with Stacy Prammanasudh's dad Lou was enlightening. Given the traits he taught, it was not hard to understand how a talented young person could reach her dream with very few resources or opportunities. He had many "words of wisdom," some of which were clichés. But for this family they were guidelines for life. He taught his daughter to be ambitious but humble. "You can go as high as you want, but keep your feet on the ground and remember where you came from." Lou Prammanasudh said. "Don't try – do it or don't do it. When you try you never give anything 110 percent. When you decide to do something, you do give it 110 percent. That's what excellence takes." Chris Riley said he was taught about commitment and persistence. "You need to be committed to do your best."

♛

## Teach your child respect for all life

**Teach him to respect the feelings, rights and property of others and respect for the game he is playing.**

The Song twins were taught respect for their elders – a common value expressed by all of the Asian juniors with whom I have worked. Respect is not a value demonstrated by so many other juniors who have been raised in the "American tradition." I know you don't want to think of yourself as an "elder" – but as a parent you are your child's elder.

Why are so many kids disrespectful to their parents?

+ They see disrespect at home or in their friends' homes.

+ They have not been taught appropriate behavior.

+ When kids are frustrated by their parent's unwillingness to listen or acknowledge them they use rude behavior to get attention.

Good manners are a way of showing respect for others. David Balbi, 1999 Northern California PGA Teacher of the Year said he has "fired" juniors for lack of respect. "I refuse to work with kids who are rude to me or their parents," he said.

♛

## Teach your child the concept of respect for himself

To do this you must treat him with respect. He cannot learn respect for himself if you call him names, embarrass him in public, don't listen to his opinions and discount the opinions he does express.

♛

# Teach your child that she is a member of a family and community and not the center of the universe

Of course when she was born she was the center of the universe. But between ages two and three she should be learning that other people have needs and rights. If you continue to act as if whole world revolves around her wishes, she will continue to believe it does. Very often talented kids do get priority and more than their share of family resources. A real champion accepts the fact that there is just so much time, energy and money available, and that family life is a process of give and take. Sometimes you can't or won't be able to take your child to a tournament. Sometimes the budget doesn't allow for new equipment. If there are siblings, they deserve time attention and resources, too. And believe it or not, parents also deserve a life.

♔

# Teach your child gratitude

People who regularly play golf are privileged. Golf is the most expensive sport one can play. To play at the highest level, your junior needs lessons, good equipment and the family must have the financial resources for tournaments and travel. Dennis Beljan, father of 2002 U.S. Junior Champion Charlie Beljan, said, "If you don't have the finances, you're not going to make it." Tournament venues are visual delights and generally in neighborhoods of large, lovely homes. People who are used to a life that includes golf tend to take it for granted. Perhaps even you do. It's important to expose juniors to "real life" – not just the fantasies and tragedies they see on television.

It's a wise parent who can compassionately teach her child that all human beings have hopes and dreams and feelings, but that unfortunately few people have the opportunities to easily live their dreams. Give your child a perspective that encourages her to appreciate and value what she has. (Hint: Avoid teaching this lesson in a way that induces guilt. Do not mention how hard you had it as a child, how spoiled she is, etc.) If you often talk sincerely about your sense of gratitude and appreciation, and if you are able to demonstrate gratitude in a tangible way, your child will grow up learning gratitude. A tangible way to demonstrate gratitude is to talk about how grateful you are, and to be charitable to those less fortunate. Remember, golf is a game that focuses on giving. Your child can learn gratitude by sharing and "giving back."

In *GolfWorld* (Aug. 13, 2004), Bill Fields writes about 9-year-old Drew Johnson, an avid junior golfer and winner of a number of trophies, who spends his Monday nights at a driving range helping a group of Special Olympic athletes. "It means a lot more to me than winning a trophy," Drew said. "When I win a trophy it's nice, but when I'm helping people, it makes me really feel good."

"Golf can be so self-absorbing and self-centered," Drew's dad Phil Johnson said. "I want my kids to reach out beyond themselves. I'd rather raise good people than great golfers."

**The latest research on happiness indicates that gratitude and kindness – or, giving to others – provides the highest level of happiness. (*Time Magazine* , Jan. 17, 2005). All the parents I interviewed said they want their children to be happy. Teaching gratitude will do more to insure happiness than anything acquired with money.**

# Teach your child how to accept disappointment and use it constructively

No one, not even the world's best golfer, wins every time. In 2004 Vijay Singh, No. 1 in the World, won nine times, but he played 29 tournaments. That's a 33 percent win rate. Tiger Woods won nine tournaments in 2000 but played in 20 (45 percent win rate). In 2004, the world's best woman player, Annika Sorenstam, had eight wins in 18 starts on the LPGA Tour and three more international wins for a total of 11. Most professional golfers have never won a tournament. In professional golf, half the field gets cut after two rounds. Just playing on the weekend is a victory of sorts.

There are parents who emphasize winning so much that their children feel like failures if they don't get a trophy: "He gets very upset and cries if he doesn't get a trophy," said the father of a 7 year-old. I've heard that kind of comment too often. When you stress or even suggest that winning is the only goal, your child is in for much bitter disappointment. Many older juniors feel inadequate or like failures if they are not among the top few in their age group. That feeling is likely to have a detrimental impact on their future performance and has a definite negative impact on self-esteem.

The best thing you can do for your child is to emphasize the pleasure of playing his best. He should have fun and not give up. With that attitude there is always a chance of birdies on the last few holes. Many professional tournaments are won by the players who come from far behind. Help your child understand that golf is a difficult and fickle game; even though he tries his hardest and plays well, most of the time he will not finish first. But each round is an opportunity to learn something. Emphasize that learning can be considered "winning," since the more one learns, the better one plays – and ultimately, the better one lives. Every improvement is a victory, even if one is "below the cut line." The player who loves the game will be motivated to inch his way onto and up the leader board.

♛

## Teach your child to be resourceful and self-sufficient

If you do everything for your child he will always be dependent or have feelings of entitlement. Everyone should be able to take care of themselves when they reach adulthood. Many children are raised to believe that all they have to do is want something and it magically appears.

I am a great believer in what I call "sharing responsibility for the household." Other people label this chores. It is my belief that people need to make a contribution in exchange for a home to live in, food, clothes, toys, golf clubs and lessons, and, for older kids, cars. A number of parents told me that schoolwork and golf practice are time consuming enough, and they don't ask their kids for anything else. There is not a child on the planet who is so busy that he can't contribute a little time to the household or family – even 30 minutes a week can teach the concept of fair exchange. Children learn by participation and how to run a household is an essential skill. You might argue, "My child will make so much money as a pro he'll have others to handle the details of his life." Don't count on it. At the very least he will have to be skillful enough to manage all those people.

♛

# Your child should learn to make decisions

It's easy to tell your children exactly what to do; but then they will never learn how to think for themselves – a real problem when you are not with them. Encourage them to look at alternatives and make choices. You can always guide or veto those choices if they are unwise.

Playing golf is a wonderful teaching tool from which to learn evaluating, reasoning, decision making, emotional control, cause and effect. I discussed a mutual junior client with his teaching pro, who told me the child is incredibly talented, can do anything he is asked to do with the club and balls, but he can't think for himself. His father is always thinking for him and telling him exactly what to do. Then after tournaments in which the father can't caddy, he berates his son for not using his head. He has never given him the opportunity to learn how to do that.

♛

# Teach your children some basics about money

Competing, especially on the national level, costs money. My client Bart had just returned from a two-day trip to take a lesson with one of the top teaching professionals in the country, and had recently been fitted with new clubs. I knew that there were other children in the family and that both parents were working. Bart wanted to go on a ski trip with his friends on the weekend. His father said "no." The phrase "it's too expensive" meant nothing to Bart. He felt deprived because his friends' parents were allowing them to go.

When I talked to Bart it became clear that his parents had

never talked to him about money. It just seemed to flow whenever he wanted anything golf related. I explained the concept of money to him using a pie chart.

- Mom and Dad work to earn money; there is just so much per month for the whole family to live on.

- This part of the pie goes to the mortgage, electricity and phone, this part goes to food, this part goes to the cars, clothes, dentists, etc.

- This part of the pie is left for everyone in the family to share.

- The trip to see the teaching pro and your new clubs have used up your share this month.

Bart was still unhappy that he couldn't go skiing, but at least he understood his parents' refusal and learned a little about an essential life skill: budgeting.

An outstanding resource to educate children about finances is Dr. Judith Briles' book *"Smart-Money Moves for Kids."*

♔

## Teach your child to manage his time for life balance

One of my young professional clients requested help planning his time to be tournament ready each time he teed up. He needed guidance scheduling his tournament weeks to include practice, physical workouts, rest and rejuvenation. The weeks he was not on the road he also needed to schedule his limited time to his best advantage. It was too easy to for him to default into watching television or activities suggested by others.

When I asked young golfers what their parents could have done that would have been especially helpful, Kyle Gentry, who is on the Stanford University golf team, said that he wished he had learned about goal-setting and planning earlier. That would have made practice and school easier. He said it is hard for juniors to discipline themselves and get schoolwork and practice done and use free time effectively.

Erik Eidsmo asked me for references to teach time management, prioritizing and planning to young people who have heavy play, practice and homework schedules.

During the 1980s, I developed and taught time management and life balance programs to business people, conducting seminars in more than 450 cities throughout the U.S., Canada, Australia and the United Kingdom. I have rewritten this material and adapted it to young people with demanding schedules. It is available on CD and as simple worksheet supplements to this book. (see order page)

♛

## Teach tour child healthy habits

Good habits include eating regular nourishing meals. Of course you must set the example and have the right kinds of food in the house. Aree Song said one of her mother's roles was to keep the family healthy, while Matt Garcia said one of the best things his mother does for him is to see to it that he has a good breakfast before he plays. It all comes down to the whole family living a physically and mentally healthy lifestyle.

👑

This list of things to teach your children is never complete. You will be teaching them long after they are out on their own. Think about what kind of adult you want to raise and add appropriate lessons to this list. If you've done a good job parenting, eventually your children will come to you to discuss career opportunities, raising their children or helping with some financial decisions. Your goal in the long run is to have children who respect you and trust your judgment.

**The real payoff comes when you can go to your children for advice because you trust their judgment. That confirms that you have done a good job.**

---

**IMPORTANT NOTE: When teaching your children, never do it when you are angry. Instead, sit down with them and teach life lessons when your anger has dissipated and you can be rational and calm about the topic of the lesson.**

---

# ACTION IDEAS

There are numerous topics in this section so I am giving you several action ideas:

## ACTION IDEA #1

**Make a list of the questions I pose in this section, and answer them thoughtfully.**

## ACTION IDEA #2

**Keep a gratitude journal.** A number of researchers on moods, especially happiness, came to the same conclusion. They discovered that when people express gratitude, or do kind acts, their life satisfaction increases. Get a nice journal at a stationary store for each member of the family. Each of you should write down at least three things you are grateful for each day. (They do not have to be different every day) At the end of the day, each family member can read something on the gratitude list to the family.

> *"Gratitude exercises can do more than lift one's mood. At the University of California Davis psychologist Robert Emmons found they improve physical health, raise energy levels, relieve pain and fatigue. The ones who benefited the most tended to elaborate more and have a wider span of things they're grateful for."*
> *– (Time Magazine,* Jan. 17, 2005)

## ACTION IDEA #3

**Have a family values discussion.** Generally, children learn values through observation and assimilation. To make sure your values are clear to your children, make a list of your values and involve your children in a discussion of specific actions to take to live those values.. The following example will give you a start.

# OUR FAMILY VALUES

**Honesty:**

We avoid little white lies– they can easily become grey or black

We always return things to their rightful owner.

Others _____

_____

**Family First**

We attend events that are important to family members.

We don't make demeaning remarks about family members to others, or embarrass them.

We 'treat our loved one's like strangers.'

Others _____

_____

**Education**

We consider school events and homework priorities

We encourage all family members to read and learn new things.

Others _____

_____

# ACTION IDEA #4

**Read Dr. Judith Briles book *Smart-Money Moves for Kids*.**

# ACTION IDEA #5

**Order the *Time Management and Life Balance for Young People* CD and worksheet supplement to this book and do the exercises. (See order page.)**

# PART III:
## MORE THOUGHTS ON PARENTING

### Nurturing creative genius

Every infant is born with innate creativity. I'm going to borrow a concept from Wayne Dyer, author of more than 20 books on self-development, and use the phrase "creative genius." You might not have given much though to this, but if you carefully watch the development of infants you have to marvel at their ability to learn about their environment and how to communicate before they have language skills and while their environment is limited to their homes, strollers and car seats.

When my children were young I was so involved in the process of their physical care and the overwhelming administrative details of running a household and making a living that I did not fully appreciate the miracle of their development as unique human beings. Now I have the joyful privilege of watching three toddler grandsons learn about the world. I am truly amazed at the development of their personalities, levels of understanding, competence, and uniqueness. Even the twins, who have been side by side since the moment of conception, are expressing themselves in their own individual ways. They are a wonderful illustration of the fact that each of us is born with talents and potential beyond what we express in our daily lives.

I am amazed as I watch the twins' older cousin Jacob excel in areas totally unique to him. Each time I visit with Jacob I wonder how someone so young can be competent in so many different areas: playing the guitar, filming movies and editing them on the computer, stunt riding on dirt bikes and more. These are his passions, the result of his unique, innate "creative genius." On the other hand, he has to be "firmly encouraged" to write book reports and do school work – unlike his scholarly parents at that age.

Rudy Duran, who was Tiger Woods' first golf instructor, called Tiger "genetically superior" in terms of golfing potential. Tiger was the one who drove himself to develop that potential. His parents recognized his drive and offered him every opportunity to maximize his innate gift. Think about your child. Does he express creative genius in golf? Is it his passion? Or are you pushing him into a mold because it's the family sport, it's good for his character, it teaches discipline and integrity, it will get him a college scholarship and he can have a lucrative and glamorous career as a professional?

♛

**A child will be passionate about and self-motivated to fully develop his creative genius.** Sometimes it takes a while for that creative genius to express itself. Golf was Mike Riley's passion; as a matter of fact, Mike was the first kid in the San Diego Junior golf program. He gave up his dream of a golf career to fight in Vietnam. When his sons, Chris and Kevin, were 6 and 7, Mike took them to the driving range on alternate days so he could spend individual time with each boy sharing a sport that meant so much to him. He taught them golf by creating fun games. After golf they went to the donut shop.

Chris said he wasn't that interested in golf when he was very young, but the games and the donuts were fun. He said that when he was 10 he "got the bug." Though he played other sports, he discovered his own creative genius for golf and became self-motivated. By age 13 he had developed a love for competition. Mike told me Chris was known in San Diego as the "second best junior" (a boy named Phil Mickelson was first – Phil showed his creative genius as a toddler.)

Though Chris had no formal lessons until he was 20 (Dad taught him the basics) he was a four-time all-American at University of Nevada, Las Vegas. At 22 he was a teammate of Tiger Woods on the 1995 Walker Cup team and is a rising star on the PGA Tour. As an adult, he is a happy friendly man who loves playing golf –  and giving back to the game.

♛

**Appreciate, revel in and support your child's uniqueness and creative genius. Let him develop at his own rate.**

Reject the notion that he has to conform to peers, and stay "within the box." That might mean stop pursuing the perfect swing, providing too many lessons, scheduling so many tournaments, doing all the "right things" because that's what others his age are doing. However, it also may mean that your child is ready to learn or compete at an accelerated rate. **In either case your child must thoroughly enjoy what he is doing to fully achieve his potential.**

Tying to fit your child into the perfect mold or to compare him to others has the potential for creating serious problems in the future. For one of my pro golf tour clients, the search for perfection has made him a frustrated, anxious person whose creative genius has been buried and whose performance has deteriorated. I also find that those amateur and recreational golfers who are not scoring up to their abilities also score high in the "controlling/perfectionist" category on the mental hazard assessment I give them. This obsession with perfectionism invariably leads to focus on mechanics and much self-criticism instead of focus on playing golf. Champion golfers focus on playing golf.

♛

## About motivation

The best results in any endeavor are achieved by people who are self-motivated. Self-motivation comes when one enjoys an activity in which he has a sense of efficacy ("I can do it") is confident in his self worth ("I am a valuable human being") and is striving for a specific goal.

Dick Wedzick teaches golf at the International Junior Golf Academy on Hilton Head Island, S.C. I was surprised to get a call from him asking, "How can I motivate my 14-year-old twins to practice?" His daughters were talented young golfers who had access to the best resources, but they didn't want to practice. My answer to him was, "You can't motivate them. You could force them to practice and punish them when they don't, but that will backfire eventually. When they understand the benefits of playing well and when they want those benefits badly, they will become self-motivated and practice."

Age 14 is a difficult, generally confusing time for kids. Their interests are expanding, they want to explore. Only the most goal-oriented kids are ready to focus on one thing. Kids need to have a passion for golf and be self-motivated in order to take golf to a high level. I suggested that Dick give his daughters opportunities to play, but not to push or pressure them. Pressure has the potential of creating rebellion – a normal teenage response. Sometimes talented kids will fail to develop their talents just to defy their overbearing parents. This is a natural part of growing up.

The Wedzick twins were 17 when I interviewed the family for this book. Dick told me they had decided to practice after discovering that they enjoyed the competition of tournaments. And now they wanted to play college golf. They realized that practice was necessary to play at higher levels and achieve their goals. Thus, self-motivation – and Dad's problem solved! The motivation that leads to achievement comes from within. Sometimes, as with the Wedzick girls, it takes more time to appear. Sometimes it takes a little stimulation, as in the case of Chris Riley, while some kids just seem to be born motivated.

Matt Garcia began working with me on his mental game at 14 and promptly won a number of junior tournaments in California. He takes the initiative to call me with insightful questions more often than most of my clients. His self-motivation was evident as an infant. His mother told me that when he was 18 months old, Matt was given a little plastic toy golf club – and never put the club down. His dad told me that before long, Matt was able to hit real golf balls over the backyard fence with the toy. Matthew's fascination with golf seemed to begin even before he picked up the toy club. "Sometime as an infant, when he was fussy," his dad said, "he sat with me in front of the TV. When I channel surfed and came to golf, he would stop me on that channel. The golf would transfix him."

Corrina Rees' older sister was enrolled in a junior golf clinic. Instead of sitting in the stroller watching, or dozing, 2-year-old Corrina climbed out of her stroller and insisted on joining her sister. She actually took instruction seriously at age 2. Today she is a junior in high school, and while there is no girls' team at her school, she plays on the boy's team – and is one of the top players in the league. Her aspirations for college and professional golf are all hers. She is not pushed by her parents, who completely support and guide her in her commitment.

There are many parents who don't have the financial resources to "buy" what their child needs. However, a child with self-esteem, inner resources and motivation will find a way to succeed.

Woody Austin is an example. Woody was 45th on the PGA Tour money list in 2004, with a career that has included being medalist at Qualifying School in 1994, Rookie of the Year in 1995 and two tour wins. Growing up he had none of the privileges of lessons, good equipment, or even a place to practice. He did not become interested in golf until high school. But Woody has creative genius for sports, so he was able to teach himself golf by playing 45 holes every weekend – at a course that had no practice range. Yet Woody played college golf on a scholarship and has earned about $3 million during the 2003 and 2004 seasons. Woody's parents didn't give him lessons at age 7, or send him off to an expensive golf academy, and they certainly put no pressure on him when he played tournaments. **The moral of the story is a motivated person will do what it takes to achieve his dream – as long as it is his dream.**

A dream was pursued by Michael J. Colgan, who was born with Cerebral Palsy. As a 5-year-old, he loved riding in the golf cart when his father played. He wanted to play, too. He had a natural ability to swing the club, though his legs wouldn't carry him far enough to walk on the course. His father said his son was born with heart – the desire to reach a goal and the willingness and determination to reach that goal through hard work. His parents encouraged him and gave him every opportunity to play. M.J. has to be helped to set up, but the swing is all his. He shoots in the 70s. He won the California Special Olympics championship four times and the National Special Olympics Championship three times. Now he attends college and speaks at national events raising funds as a Global Ambassador for Special Olympics. Michael is a true champion.

♛

**A common element among those who play at the highest level is the passion and self-motivation that leads to almost "begging" to be able to play and practice at a very young age.**

Children who were pushed and pressured by overzealous parents might excel in the short run, but sadly do not perform up to their own potential in the long run. This is confirmed by the mediocre to disappointing performance of the "pushed" juniors who do make it to the professional tours.

♛

## About pressure

Kansas Gooden was a highly competitive junior when I worked with her in 1999. I interviewed her mother Connie for this book. She said, "Kids who play junior golf, especially in the highly competitive AJGA and FCWT tours are under tremendous pressure, often self-inflicted, and at other times parent inflicted. They are likely to release that stress by rudeness and lack of respect or anger at parents. I wonder if it would have been better to pay the college tuition than put my child (and family) through all the pressure associated with getting recognized by coaches at the top schools."

There is inherent pressure in any type of performance that is judged and has the potential for either reward or punishment or criticism. There is pressure for grades in school; there is pressure on the golf course in competition. Children want to please their parents, so there is the pressure of vying for approval. Since golf requires a huge investment on the parents' part, kids feel additional pressure not to disappoint parents. There is also the potential for a lot of guilt if their performance doesn't measure up to the parent's investment (especially if the parents remind the kids of how much they are sacrificing.) Your child knows that you are putting time, energy and money into his golf. You should emphasize that, "We are doing this because we love you and want to support any worthwhile activity that you are committed to. Sometimes you won't play well, but if you have fun and learn something it's worth it."

♔

There is an inverse relationship between pressure and consistent peak performance. The more pressure there is, the less likely that your child will perform well. The negative impact of pressure and stress has been extensively researched and documented since it was first identified close to 70 years ago by Hans Selye, the first person to study stress scientifically. His research proved that stress creates physiological responses in the body, including tension in the muscles, (this can lead to mechanical flaws.) Stress impacts the mind in a way that makes it difficult to concentrate and focus. The biochemical changes impact energy and, ultimately, stress weakens the immune system. Basically, pressure/stress is bad for physical and mental health and performance. I believe that Ty Tryon's mononucleosis at the onset of his professional career at age 17 was a result of more stress than a teenager was prepared to handle.

A small amount of pressure – which I call "positive stimulation" – is necessary in order to call on the mind and body's performance energy. When I was a professional speaker, one of the truisms of our business was that it is important to feel a few butterflies before a presentation (it means you care about what you are doing), but they must fly in formation. Champions care about their performance. This gives them that "positive stimulation." Many champion kids are so hard on themselves that it interferes with their best performance. They don't need any more pressure from parents. Positive encouragement is always welcome. Criticism and negative pressure are not. If you want to avoid putting unnecessary pressure on your child, seriously consider implementing the suggestions in this book.

As a stress management specialist, I recorded an audiocassette program called, "5 Days to Less Stress" in 1983 and wrote, "Stress First Aid for the Working Woman" in 1991. To supplement this book, I have adapted and updated some of this material for golfers, This new CD includes relaxation, stress reduction and anger management techniques that are useful before and during play. (Order page)

♛

## About criticism

*"If you want your children to improve, let them overhear the nice things you say about them to others."*
— Dr. Haim Ginott

**Why find fault? There's no reward offered.**

One exasperated father complained to me that his son overestimates how far he can hit his irons. The son complained, "My dad always criticizes my club selection.

Unless the shot's perfect, all my mistakes are because I don't listen to him." After a round when the son hit a beautifully executed, but short 9-iron shot on the 18th hole, I heard an angry exchange.

Father: "You wasted a shot again. You never take enough club, you kids always think you can hit farther than you can. I keep telling you to take more club and swing easier, but you're stubborn, you never listen, don't think you're such a hot shot, you're not as good as you think."

Son: "As if you know everything." (He then turned his back on his father and walked off.)

I asked the father what his tirade accomplished. "He knows where I stand," he said. My response to that was, "But you have been telling him the same thing for months. He knew where you stood six months ago. How has that changed his behavior?" I explained that a normal teenager is more likely to try to prove himself right than give in to his father. I suggested the next time, Dad might try the following strategy in a patient tone of voice:

"That was a beautiful swing with the 9 iron. Too bad the ball didn't reach the green. What can you learn about selecting the club that will put the ball where you want it?"

Will that solve the problem? It certainly has a better chance than the criticism that had a history of not working. It asks the player to think about how to correct his own errors. Many parents complain that their children make what they call "too many errors in judgment," or have poor course management. Remember, kids are not mature yet and cannot be expected to have the same kind of judgment as their parents.

If your child "makes the same mistakes over and over no

matter how many times I correct him," it is generally because you angrily point out the mistakes instead of patiently teaching him how to avoid them. Make it a habit to focus on how to avoid the same mistake in the future.

♕

**Acknowledge and reward the behavior that you want.**

I learned an important lesson from my son when he was an adolescent. It was his job to empty the wastebaskets into the garbage can the day before the garbage was collected. Invariably he would forget to empty one of the wastebaskets, leave a trail of Kleenex down the hall, or trash on the ground around the garbage can. And invariably, I would complain, "Why aren't you more careful when you are emptying the wastebaskets?" Or, "You forgot the one in the hall bathroom." One day he said, "There are seven wastebaskets in this house, I emptied six and the only thing you notice is the one I didn't get."

I asked, "What do I have to do so you will do a complete job?" He said, "You can thank me for what I did right." (Light bulb on!) Of course – that's how to improve performance. From my days of teaching business psychology, I knew that appreciation is the leading motivator for employees (a number of studies have shown that appreciation ranks significantly higher than money). So, it was a matter of putting that knowledge to use in eliciting more good behavior from my son. I began to notice what he was doing right. I found every opportunity to notice and thank my son for the behavior I wanted. "Thank you for taking your dishes to the sink." " Thank you for turning the lights out when you left your room." "Thank you for remembering….without being reminded." Did that work? Absolutely. I found my son taking initiative and being responsible for things I didn't even ask for. Ultimately, he became totally accountable for his behavior.

Even today as I watch my adult children make decisions that I would not make, I am careful not to criticize their choices. It makes for far more harmonious family relationships – and besides, it's still possible that I am the one that is in error.

**Most parents ignore what is going right and criticize what must be corrected. We get more of what we reinforce. My term for this is, "What you measure for multiplies." If you notice good behavior, it will persist or increase. If you pay more attention to what is wrong, you will get more of the same – which means if you call attention to your child's three-putts, he will get nervous on the green and his putting will probably get worse.**

♔

**Never say, "You always" or "You never" – unless attached to a compliment.**

Unfortunately, "always" and "never" are usually attached to a reprimand. "You are always late" … "You always think of yourself, you never consider others" … " I always have to remind you to take your homework to school" … "You never put down the toilet seat." These statements are not true. Often? Perhaps. Always? No. Here are some suggestions for using always and never constructively: "I know you didn't play well today, but I know you always do your best" … "You always can count on me to be there for you" … "I never will tell your secrets to other parents" … 'I always will love you, even though sometimes I won't like what you do."

♔

**Avoid attacks. They stimulate counter-attack.**

When my children do something that I think is really "stupid," my knee-jerk reaction would be to ask, "Are you out of your mind?" This is known as an attack. The likely response would be either a defense or a counter attack, neither of which is productive. However, I have learned to cool it before expressing my opinion. So, instead I say something like, "I'm not clear why you made that decision, can you explain that choice to me?" Sometimes I get a reasonable answer. If not, I can follow up with, "Have you considered ...?" and then I express my opinion. This is known as an exchange. Exchanges are likely to stimulate thinking and are an opening to influence or understanding.

♛

**Every time you criticize your child, rather than his specific behavior, you are setting the stage for undermined self-esteem, which then translates into lack of confidence.**

"You didn't read the green again ... Use your eyes, it's a fast downhill putt ... You're so careless ... Why don't you use your head? I pay a fortune for lessons and you don't learn a %@# thing from them ..." Those criticisms are likely to cause resentment and frustration. It is more helpful and more likely to get positive results if you say, "I know you were trying your best, but can I make a suggestion? Make sure you read the greens more carefully, and then you'll have a better sense of the right speed for the putt."

♛

**Finally, there's no percentage in being "right."**

Would you rather be right – and resented and ignored– or would you rather be respected and listened to? When you admit a mistake, or that you don't have all the answers, you are likely to be respected and listened to. No one respects or listens seriously to a "know it all," especially a parent "know it all." Admitting a mistake shows respect for others. Your child is more likely to admit his mistakes if he sees you modeling this desirable behavior.

♛

**To think about:**

+ How do you feel and how do you respond when you are criticized by your spouse, by your boss, or any one else in authority?

+ Do you remember how you felt and responded when you were criticized by your parents?

♛

## About listening

**The purpose of listening is to learn. When your child listens to you he should learn something about what he needs to know in order to become a responsible self-sufficient member of the larger community. When you listen to your child you should learn something about him and his needs.**

The best way to get your child to listen and consider your advice or instructions is to model the behavior you want. Steven Covey in his book, *"The Seven Habits of Highly Effective People"* states it beautifully: "Seek First to Understand, Then to be Understood."

Most conversations between parents and children involve the parents telling the children what to do, how to behave, what the parent expects, or some sort of criticism. Since this communication comes from the authority who ultimately has the last word, the children can:

1. Go with the program willingly.
2. Go with the program reluctantly – grumbling out loud or perhaps keeping their frustration to themselves.
3. Become passive-aggressive – "accidentally" causing the parents inconvenience, or embarrassment, or causing themselves harm.
4. Rebel, by defying the parents.

Given a choice, most parents would opt for alternative No. 1, with a normal sprinkling of No. 2.

♔

**Your child is far more likely to listen to you if you have a habit of listening to her.**

You may have the tendency to tell your kids, "I pay the bills and you'll do what I say, " or "I'm the parent I know what's good for you." But it shows respect and you will get better results when you fully listen to your child's point of view without criticism or counter argument. When she is finished expressing her point of view, she is much more likely to listen to you. Then you can explain your decision based on values, house rules, safety, finances, or whatever sensible reason you have. It is even possible that your final decision can be influenced by her input. **Teaching and guiding rather than commanding is a time consuming process, but will result in a child who is more likely to make wise decisions for herself when there is no parent there for guidance.**

There is a natural tendency to listen to people who share your point of view. How many Democrats are really willing to listen with an open, non-judgmental ear to Republicans, and vice-versa? I know I tend to think along party lines – and have to stop myself from forming a premature cast-in-stone position. When I listen to the other point of view, I often find merit in those positions. As an adult, it's important that you open your mind to your child's point of view. You may find your child has a valid position; at the very least you will be more understanding of it.

As the adult, can you avoid or end an argument by listening first, then considering before explaining and rendering the final decision? Most parents can't; we're too busy. We have to move the administrative business of the household forward; we have work to do, bills to pay and maybe other children in the household to consider. "Because I said so," is a fast, efficient response. But "Because I said so," doesn't cut it with anyone anymore. You can do better than that.

♛

**Listen fully without criticism or making him feel stupid.**

"That's interesting, but have you considered the consequences of …" is a better response to an irrational or untenable point of view than, "That's really stupid. What were you thinking?" If he's is a teenager, he probably wasn't thinking! (Refer back to "Avoid Attacks" in the Criticism section and "They're not finished yet" in the Introduction.)

♛

**The best way to get someone to listen to you is to open every conversation – especially one that involves something you want to correct – with something they would like to hear.**

"I notice that you are getting more patient with your brother when you go out to play. I'm pleased with that new attitude. Since you were able to be more patient with your brother, I know you can be more patient with yourself and stop banging clubs when you miss a shot. That is inappropriate behavior, you know."

That might be enough to get results, but you can follow up with consequences if necessary. (See the section on discipline.)

♛

**Pose questions instead of making statements.**

"I'm paying a fortune for lessons and you don't pay attention to what your pro teaches you." That is a statement that is not likely to get the results you want. Instead try something like, "Is there something you don't understand about what the pro taught you last week?" Or, "Is there something I can do to help you get the most benefit from your lessons?"

"You've got to practice more if you expect to get better," will likely get the following response from a teenager: "I know, I know," – ignore. Instead, try, "Do you have so much homework that you don't have time to practice?" Or, "Have you changed your mind about wanting to be No. 1 on the team?" Those are the type questions that provide an opening for a non-emotional discussion of the reason practice has fallen off. You then can talk about the relationship between practice and consistent results or the importance of practicing the short game.

♛

**Let go of, "What's the matter with you?"**

If you consistently ask that question, your child will begin to believe there really is something wrong with him. Focus on "I know you have what it takes, but now you're not living up to your potential. How can I help you reach your goals?"

☗

**Speak softly.**

Yelling creates the desire to tune out the yeller. It also invites counter-yelling and a lot of non-constructive noise. When you yell, it means you have lost control. A person who speaks softly has more power. When you speak softly, the listener must make an effort to pay attention. That's what you want – you want your kids to pay attention. Speaking softly implies self-control, a good trait to instill in your child. The person who speaks softly generally speaks more slowly and considers his words more carefully. This leads to fewer words you might regret.

☗

**Measure your words.**

If you keep up a constant stream of directions and instructions you are likely to be tuned out. I have heard parents bombard their kids with a long list of "Dos and Don'ts" before or after a tournament. No mind can process that much information. It's easier to ignore it all. The more you tell them to do, the less likely they will listen.

If one of my tour professional clients has not scored well, he listens to about one sentence of his father's post-round phone message and deletes the rest, commenting to me, "He always says the same thing,... I've heard this over and over." If he misses a cut, he doesn't listen to this father's message at all.

Communication from you should build up your child, teach him how to achieve his potential, inculcate values, express your love, and support and prepare him to be a champion.

♛

## About discipline

**The purpose of discipline is to teach children to make good choices – it is not to inflict pain.**

Discipline involves knowing and living by rules and guidelines. Your child should know what behavior is expected and acceptable. This gives him guidelines for making decisions. A disciplined child knows there are consequences for behavior. There should be a reward for good behavior. This can be as simple as a "Thank You," a smile, or hug. Parents should make sure there are undesirable consequences for bad behavior. Examples are "time out" from the course, grounding, taking away privileges, or other appropriate penalties. After all, in golf tournaments there are inherent consequences of undesirable behavior such as a stroke penalty, or disqualification.

Discipline teaches responsibility, self-control and respect. Discipline can originate externally (from parents, teachers, rules officials), or internally. The ideal is that the child learns self-discipline so he can make decisions that will lead to the satisfying productive life of a champion. Remember, the definition of a champion is a human being who fulfills his potential and lives a life of satisfaction and service. Trophies are only a bonus.

♛

**Punishment involves inflicting pain – either physical or emotional.**

Emotional pain can last a lot longer than physical pain. Inflicting pain will work temporarily, since behavior generally improves for a while for fear of more punishment. However punishment results in resentment, the desire to get even and sets the stage for dishonesty. Long term, punishment backfires on the punisher and has serious life consequences for the person raised with fear and pain. Research tells us that people raised with harsh and unfair punishment suffer serious emotional and social problems in adult life.

**You can look at discipline (and/or punishment) as being on a continuum of family "styles," from Parent-Centered to Child-Centered. In the middle is the Collaborative style.**

1 — 2 — 3 — 4 — 5 — 6 — 7 — 8 — 9 — 10
Parent Centered        Collaborative        Child Centered

In a parent centered home (1, 2, 3), the parents make the rules and punish the child for infractions. Sometimes the child doesn't know the rules in advance. He just does something wrong and the parent punishes him. The punishment in this type of home can be arbitrary and overly harsh. Sometimes the child does know the rules – and the punishment is still harsh. Bill Fields wrote in *GolfWorld* (Sept. 12, 2003) about a parent who makes his son run a mile for every stroke over 75. Another parent is known for abandoning his child at the tournament site when she didn't play well. Eventually, parents at the low number end of the discipline continuum are not likely to raise champions. They may raise kids who earn a trophy or two, but in the long run, the price paid is too high.

There are extreme child-centered families (8, 9, 10), where

discipline and punishment are nonexistent. In these homes the child can get away with anything. The parents feel somewhat helpless, as they often support the child's bad behavior.

One such permissive father playing golf with his daughter grumbled as he filled her divots and repaired ball marks and otherwise cleaned up after her. "I keep telling her to leave the course in better condition than she found it. Why can't she learn to take care of these things herself?" he asked. "Why should she?" I replied. "She sees you doing it for her. Tell and show her what is expected and let her know that if she doesn't respect the course, you will take her off the course. After one warning, follow through." I had no expectation that he would follow my advice. This was the same child who earlier had gotten a new jacket in the pro shop because she "forgot" hers and filled up on junk food in the cafe because she didn't like the lunch she was served at home.

Two years later, the same father was again complaining about his daughter. She had given up golf and was now under the influence of peers whose values were inconsistent with the family value of education. He said he no longer had influence over her. I suggested that he had had no influence over her for years.

I get many complaints from parents who do too much for their children and then get upset when the kids are careless, disrespectful and irresponsible. The extreme child centered home will produce a self-centered, high-maintenance, demanding or irresponsible adult, not a champion.

**Collaborative style families have the greatest chance of producing champions.**

In collaborative homes, discussions of cause and effect or the consequences of behavior is frequent. The child has choices:

"You can have fun going to the movies with your friends today, but then you will have to do your book report tomorrow so you and won't be able to go to the golf course. Which would you prefer – the movies or the golf course."

The book report is not negotiable and the child understands why. He has been well trained in the family values and education is high on the list.

♔

"My parents taught me that my life was up to me," said Kyle Gentry, when we met for the first time in several years. It was a pleasure catching up with Kyle during his winter break. He was attending Stanford University on a golf scholarship and playing on the golf team. A few minutes into my interview, it became obvious that he was a champion human being. I worked with Kyle when he took an interest in the mental game at 13. At that time his goal was the PGA Tour. Now, eight years later, he still had his goal of playing on the tour after college, but said he intended to take the law school entrance exam in case he didn't cut it as a professional golfer.

We discussed discipline in the Gentry household. "There were rules and consequences," Kyle said. "My parents made it clear that all my actions had consequences and I was responsible for my outcomes. If I didn't do my homework, I knew I would have problems in school and that would thwart my goals of college golf and then the PGA. My parents never forced me to practice. I learned from experience that if I didn't practice before a tournament my game wouldn't be sharp, I'd play poorly and I wouldn't feel good about myself. I always knew there were consequences. Then I could make a decision about whether I wanted to hang out with my friends watch TV, or practice putting. I found out that playing well was always the best outcome for me so I learned to make the right choices."

At one point in the conversation, Kyle said he was spoiled. "What makes you say that?" I asked. "My parents gave me every opportunity," he said. "I had good coaches and equipment, they took me to tournaments. They supported me in every way." I reminded Kyle that he had "earned" it with his diligence at school, with practice and by making decisions that resulted in those rewards – and that is not spoiled. "Spoiled is when your parents do everything for you while not requiring anything from you and tolerating bad behavior."

♛

Almost every parent I spoke to said their child's room was the greatest area of frustration. Living in a messy room is a normal part of the growing up process. As Kyle said, "That was the only way I could rebel without hurting myself." You will not teach your kids anything useful by either grounding them, or giving up and cleaning their room yourself. The best solution is to close the door so you don't see the mess.

Your child will learn a lot if collaboratively you make her totally responsible for her belongings: " Dirty clothes go in the hamper. If they are on your floor you won't have clean clothes to wear. If your clothes are mistreated, you won't get new clothes until you learn to care for what you have.

If it's in your room and you can't find it, no one will help you look for it or buy you another one."

**Teaching children responsibility, self-respect and self-discipline early will avoid many serious problems.**

Even a young child can be taught that behavior has consequences. In my household we had a lost and found. The kids knew that if their toys or other belongings were left in the living room or outside at the end of the day, they would end up in the lost and found – from which their things could be redeemed with work. "After you sweep the patio, you can have your tennis racquet back." That sure beat nagging them to pick up after themselves, or getting so frustrated that I threatened a harsh punishment on which I couldn't follow through. **Never threaten a consequence that you are unwilling to carry out.**

♛

Discipline through consequences takes patience. It may not get the immediate behavior change you want, but it prevents the potential psychological damage from physical punishment or verbal abuse. Discipline teaches long-term responsibility, self-reliance, pride and self-esteem. It builds champions.

You can create an effective discipline system based on golf. Golf is a game with specific rules. The purpose of the rules is to give everyone a fair opportunity, to test their skills and to avoid conflict. A golfer knows exactly what will happen if he does not follow the rules. There are stroke penalties for balls out of bounds, or in the water. There are warnings first and then penalties for slow play and, ultimately, disqualification for a more serious type of "misbehavior" such as signing in an inaccurate scorecard. The system works well because:

- The rules were decided upon in advance and they are in writing.

- Every golfer has access to and is responsible for knowing the rules.

- Rules are impersonal. The penalty is for the infraction, not the person, it's the behavior that is punished. The severity of the discipline is not dependent upon the rules official's frustration level.

You can set up such a system in your home. Using the collaborative style, discuss as a family various kinds of misbehavior and appropriate "penalties." Your children are much more likely to buy into the system if they participate in determining the rules and consequences than if you make the rules and impose them.

♛

**Never make practice a punishment.**

Both playing golf and practicing should always be seen as a desirable activity and fun. A serious golfer will want to practice because it helps her become a better player. She sees the intrinsic reward in practice. If your child had a really bad putting day and you are frustrated with her score, do not yell, "You go out and practice putting until you sink 20 in a row from three, four and six feet." She feels badly enough about her performance. **You do not want your child practicing when she is in a negative mood.**

You can however, deprive your child of golf for misbehavior. (Tida Woods used the threat of no golf as a way to keep Tiger in line.) Here you are taking away something she loves – that type of discipline works. "You know that it's unacceptable to treat your mother with such disrespect and you know the penalty for that is to come off the course. Let's go." Again, the child must know the negative consequences of bad behavior in advance.

♔

**Never "punish" a child for playing poorly.**

As young Ben Salk said, "Some kids parents that get mad and yell at kids when they don't play well. I don't get it. Don't they know they're not doing it on purpose?" It is acceptable to discipline poor sportsmanship, or giving up. But when the swing's not working the child is disappointed enough. If the child is playing poorly on purpose, there is a reason. It would make sense to explore that reason.

♔

# About lessons

I hadn't worked with Jeanine (not her real name) in 6 months. There was no need. She had been using the audio-cassette tapes I made for her – so she could work on her mental game without me – and her game had steadily improved. She was shooting in the low 70s, well enough to make a decent showing in junior tournaments, win at the local and regional level and secure a college golf scholarship. Then a frantic phone call from her mother told me she shot 98 in an important tournament and that lately she was coming in close to last every time she competed. Jeanine had stopped listening to her mental training tapes and instead had become obsessed with her swing. I asked her mother how often she had a lesson. "Every week," I was told. I thought Jeanine probably had interjected too many mechanical thoughts into her mind and was no longer able to swing freely. Her good swing had been working, but now too much focus on perfecting it had a negative impact on her game.

I first met Jeanine three years before. She had a beautiful free flowing swing. In an effort to go the next level with her game, she began to take lessons from a highly regarded teacher. It was not the right teacher for her, so instead of improving, her swing became mechanical and her game fell apart. I worked with her on some mental skills. She relaxed and the swing that produced middle of the fairway shots returned immediately. Now, three years later, she was back with a mechanical, unreliable swing as the result of weekly lessons. However, by now the stakes had become high. She needed to arrive on the college campus in the fall with the game that impressed the coach in the first place. We resumed mental training. I made her an updated self-hypnotic audiocassette that will reduce her anxiety, relax her muscles, bring back her confidence and help her to play to her potential. She decided to see her swing coach less frequently and turn her focus from trying to perfect a good swing, to playing the game with confidence and joy.

♔

I have worked with a junior who had lessons from as many as five different swing coaches in less than a year. This is an invitation for disaster. There must be a consistency in instruction and training. There is no way to integrate so much information from so many instructors and produce a consistent repeatable swing. This junior did not put enough energy into the other elements of the game. He minimized the importance of learning course management and the nuances of the short game. **The mental stamina to chip from the rough and then sink the putt when under pressure will win far more tournaments than perfect swings mechanics.**

I discussed creative genius earlier. Wayne Dyer, says each of us is born with some creative genius. Musical prodigies, math whizzes and other young talents get recognition for their genius. But according to Dyer, genius and creativity take many forms, most not classified as genius. Many young golfers are identified as having natural talent – or genius. I think it is a shame that some of that creative talent is being forced into a mechanical mold by teachers who insist they have the answer to the perfect golf swing. (As a matter of fact, each of these swing systems was created by a golfer who found a way to make the swing work. for him) Consider what would happen if you encouraged your child to explore, experiment and "play" more instead of always "working" on his swing. That is how Phil Mickelson became the No. 1 junior of his era.

### Choose the right teacher for your child.

The right teacher for your child is not necessarily the one with the best reputation, or one of America's "Top 50."

+ The best teacher for your child is one who "connects" with him.

+ The right teacher knows how children learn.

+ The right teacher can teach concepts and coach in a way the child can understand.

+ He teaches at the right pace for your child.

+ He makes learning fun.

✦ He gives positive reinforcement or rewards.

✦ The best teacher knows how to encourage improvement rather than point out mistakes.

Paul Creamer told me, "Paula was a gymnast and dancer and very social young girl. When a group of her friends decided to enroll in a junior golf clinic, she joined them. When she got serious about wanting to play more, I insisted that lessons be fun. I researched teachers to find the right one for her. The teacher I found gave the children rewards when they hit a good shot."

♛

Before committing to lessons, observe the teacher giving a lesson to another child. If this is not possible, commit to only one lesson and observe it yourself. After the lesson, determine if your child is excited and happy. Has she learned something, or is she confused? There are some teachers who are so mechanical that the child experiences nothing but frustration from lessons. Listen to how the teacher is speaking to your child. Instruction must be age-appropriate. I have observed pros give a clinic for children using terminology that only an experienced golfer would understand. After a session with a very talented 6-year-old, his father told me, "You are the first coach that has talked to him as child."

Golf is a game to enjoy. Enjoyment fosters creativity and the desire to spend time getting better. Struggling to perfect mechanics prematurely makes golf "work" and creates counter-productive frustration. As your junior matures he will require more advanced instruction. Kyle Gentry told me that when he seriously wanted to perfect his game, he looked at what was missing and took a personal interest in filling the gaps. That's when he was able to understand mechanics with the right teacher. Don't let the teacher's name determine your choice. The father of a highly ranked junior told me that his daughter took a lesson from several prominent teachers before finding one that explained things in a way that she could understand and implement. This is the very same teacher that others have criticized for being too mechanical and rigid – but the approach suits this particular junior's learning style and needs. He's the right teacher for her.

♛

I worked on the mental game with the son of a highly regarded teaching professional. The son had tour aspirations and the father had the same expectations for his son. Dad had coached several successful touring professionals and high-performing amateurs who thought he was a wonderful coach. His learning system and teaching style worked for his students. It didn't work for his son. The son had a different learning style. I observed the arguments and struggles between father who was so successful with his students, and the son who had great difficulty learning the way his father taught. The more the father explained things "his way" the less the son could "do it right."

You've heard some golfers say they are "feel" golfers. It's a lost cause to talk to them about physics and expect that to improve their performance. They learn about physics by experimenting with feel first. Some coaches talk far too much for students who learn by watching and doing. And other people learn best with a great deal of information that they can then process.

There are many different communication and learning styles – and as many evaluation tools for determining each person's style. Some coaches and sports psychologists administer versions of these evaluations. I found these devices extremely helpful when I was teaching business psychology and communication skills. An understanding of styles fosters effective communication. These tools help employers fit people into the right job and manage them well. The tools are used extensively in sales training and are extremely helpful for diffusing and even avoiding interpersonal conflict. An understanding of learning and communication styles can make golf instruction far more effective, and most important, help parents find the right coach for their children. (See references for more information.)

♛

Left to their own devices, motivated passionate kids will experiment with golf clubs and golf balls to determine what they can do with them. Phil Mickelson did not learn his incredible flop shot and other "trick shots" – like the backward over-his-head bunker shot that he demonstrated at the 2003 AT&T Pebble Beach Pro-Am – from a swing coach. He learned through this joy in experimentation and discovery. He never had to be encouraged to practice or work; he spent his time playing "with" golf. Today, too many kids are not having fun. Instead of "discovering," they are told exactly what to do and how to do it. It has become a mechanical process. It has become work. There is so much emphasis on the "right way" to swing. Do you remember the old TV commercial which featured a child asking, "Is it soup yet?" Instead of having fun, I can envision a young golfer asking, "Is it a swing yet?"

I asked one of my most serious junior clients, "Are you modeling yourself after a prominent professional golfer?" I think it's important for kids with goals to have a role model. She mentioned a male golfer. "Isn't there someone on the LPGA Tour you would like to model yourself after?" I asked. After some hesitation, I suggested Annika

Sorenstam. My client shook her head and said, "I don't like her swing." Sorenstam at 34 is a Hall of Famer who bested Tiger Woods' record in 2003 and 2004, shot 59 in a competitive round, and won 56 times in only 11 seasons. Yet this junior's rejection of her as a role model was based on the look of her swing. My concern for this junior (who is already a champion in her own right) is that her commitment to perfection will make it hard to be happy with herself – and she may be focusing on the wrong priority.

♛

Woody Austin never had a lesson. He told me that he works things out himself. One might argue that if he had lessons, he might have had more than two wins since 1995 – but maybe not. Chris Riley did not take his first formal lesson from a swing coach until age 20. They are not the only well-known professional golfers who had no instruction, or little instruction, from prominent teachers. One client picked up golf clubs at age 15, had a total of two formal lessons, and then was playing to a handicap of plus-2 within five years. He told me he just enjoyed figuring things out for himself.

♛

The best advice I can offer you is: **Make sure the teacher and lessons you choose are right for your child.** How do you know?
+ Your child likes the lessons and the teacher.
+ Your child understands and can implement what he learns.
+ Your child shows progress with lessons.
+ The teacher is focused on what the child needs rather than what the teacher wants to teach.

♛

# About Tournaments

My advice here is predominantly for parents who want a good relationship with happy, well adjusted children who will perform to the best of their ability when they compete. If your goal is a college golf scholarship, public recognition and a professional career for your child, you will probably ignore much of this advice. Just be aware that pushing and pressuring your child ultimately will backfire. Many professionals and a number of the golf writers I spoke to all agree that they have seen many kids who were pushed early reach college age and just quit playing golf.

♛

## Tournament scheduling.

One parent told me, "I let him play so much that he got exhausted and played very poorly at the end of the season." Another said, "I didn't let her play enough to achieve her point goals. I think that was a mistake." Each child has a certain amount of physical and mental stamina. The parents have just so much time and money. Tournament scheduling is a good time to collaborate. It's wise to have an overview of an entire season and coordinate that with school schedules. Your child's goals and priorities and physical and mental heath must factor into the schedule, too.

♛

## Show faith in your child's ability.

If your child wants to play tournaments, support and encourage him. Do not question his ability or hint that he hasn't practiced or worked hard enough to handle the competition at a high level. Your faith in him and his ability will bolster his self-esteem so that he can play his best.

Your child needs to feel your support before, during and after the tournament. Avoid arguments, criticism, or any negative communication that will stay with your child as he plays. Coaching on the range or putting green should be only positive reinforcement. He needs to step up to the first tee feeling good about himself, knowing that his parents believe in and support him.

♛

**Emphasize the purpose of the tournament is have fun competing, gain tournament experience and test skill levels against other young golfers.**

The goal is to play the best round possible. Winning is a bonus. Yes, tournament performance does have an impact on college scholarships, but that must be a secondary purpose. You don't want performance anxiety to sabotage play. 17 year-old Christina Stockton loves to compete. She did not have the expectation of winning the California Women's Amateur in 2004, but it was her goal to test herself against some of the best women golfers in the state – many of whom started playing golf long before Christina was born. She had a good time with her caddy – her mother, teaching pro Jolene Stockton, who was encouraging and supportive. Christina was happy to make it to the quarterfinals. It was a confidence builder for Christina and good experience for mother and daughter. Mission accomplished.

♛

**No swing lessons between tournament rounds or a few days before the tournament.**

Jeanine's coach made a small change in her swing during a lesson on a Tuesday. She traveled to a tournament Wednesday. On Thursday she shot 98, about 22 strokes higher than her recent scoring average. She told me she was trying to implement the minor adjustment made on Tuesday. Any contact with a teaching pro the week before a tournament should only be to reinforce and confirm what the junior has already been practicing. Corrina Rees says she cuts off new instruction two weeks before a tournament so she can groove in what she learned.

♛

**Physical comfort and health are important.**

Mother and teaching pro Jolene Stockton suggests that children not play in inclement weather when they are young. They should be comfortable, not too cold, or too hot, their eyes protected from glare and their skin protected from sun damage. Corinna Rees is only 16, but notices she loses focus if she is hungry, so she makes sure she has healthy nourishment with her. One mother told me her child went out to play having eaten only half a sandwich and could hardly make it through 18 holes – playing poorly on the back nine – not a good use of time, energy and tournament fees. Never allow your child play in tournaments when she is sick or injured. Six months of rehabilitation is too high a price to pay.

♛

**Stay out of the way.**

Let your child know this is her game and she is responsible for how she plays. At junior tournaments, coaching signals are a "no-no," but it is surprising how many parents do it. As a matter of fact, it was an issue with fathers on the LPGA Tour in 2003. It's not necessary to hide behind trees while watching your child – if you can control your emotions and body language. Paul Creamer laughs when he tells the story of kicking a rock when Paula hit a bad shot, and then having Paula reprimand him for it. He says it taught him to pay more attention to emotional control.

♛

**"Your actions speak so loudly, I can't hear what you are saying."**

The mother of one of my pro tour clients said, "He told me he felt good about his putting, but when he walked toward the green his shoulders were slumped and he didn't have that spring in his step. I knew he had lost confidence." You can tell just by looking, how your child feels – and your child is even more sensitive to your body language. Your child will be looking at you often to gauge your responses. "I could tell by looking at my dad that he was mad when I missed that putt on 12," said Bart, whose game fell apart on the next four holes as the picture of his father's head-shaking grimace stuck in his head.

When your child is competing, make sure your expression is either pleasantly neutral, or approving. The physical expression of impatience, anger or criticism is sure to neg-atively effect your child's enjoyment of competition and performance. When your child hits a bad shot and you turn and stomp away, you send more negative messages than your child can handle when his goal is to play his best. Arms crossed over your chest is generally interpreted as anger or impatience, though it can also mean you are cold. But if you cross your arms and purse your lips when your child is not playing well, he won't think you're cold.

**At home, have a discussion of body language and signals with your child. Ask him what your actions say to him – and what type of body language, or actions would be the most helpful to him when he is competing.**

**Remember, a number does not always indicate the quality of play.**

Bad breaks or one bad hole can make great play seem mediocre. Tara Chappell, one of my junior clients, opened her round at the high school regional championships with a four-putt. On the second tee she was already 4-over-par. However, she shot 40 on the front nine. She was able to ignore that opening 8 to play a good round. Her final score however, didn't reflect the quality of her play and superior mental stamina.

**Discuss scores as an after-thought.**

After a round, your first comment should be, "I saw some really nice shots there, tell me which ones you were especially pleased with." If your child is pleased with her play, join her in her excitement. If she is not pleased, tell her you know she tried her best, everyone has disappointing days. Emphasize that she's still a great kid and is improving.

**Use the tournament experience as aa indicator of the skills to focus on before the next competition.**

Golf is a complex game with an enormous number of variables. You and your child will find a number of different elements that need work. It's best to focus on improving one thing at a time. One can't improve a swing, putting and bunker play in the few weeks (or days) between tournaments. Chose one thing and concentrate on it. If that has improved by the next tournament, good; if not, stay with that one thing until improvement is noticeable. Then move on to the next element of the game that needs work. The truth about golf is that it is never perfect, even at the highest professional level, so there will always be things to improve upon – one thing at a time.

♛

## About practice

Children love to explore and learn. If you watch an infant with a puzzle or a toy, he will be absorbed in manipulating it. And even though he has no conscious understanding of learning or practice, he will keep manipulating that toy until he can master it. The same principle holds true for a child who has fun playing golf. All of the champions I have spoken to said they loved to practice. Harry Cathrea said his 9-year-old daughter Casie wakes him up in the morning with, "Come on dad, let's go hit balls." Golf writer John Strege told me when he was sitting on the porch interviewing Earl Woods, he could hear Tiger practice chipping around the house.

Those children who have goals to play on their high school team, play college golf, or perhaps play professionally know that they must have a certain skill level to accomplish those goals. They will be self-motivated to improve through practice and test their skills in tournaments. Even the most dedicated golfer has times when he doesn't want to practice. Perhaps your child is temporarily overloaded with schoolwork, or is low on physical or mental energy. Everyone needs a break now and then. But the committed child will miss practicing and be ready to go out again soon.

**If you the parent must constantly push or remind your child to practice and he generally resists or grumbles,**

then "golf greatness" is probably your dream and not your child's. If your child has no interest in practice, but does want to go out and play golf with his friends, let that be enough. Recognize and accept that for him golf is a pastime, not a passion, nor a future profession.

♛

Practice means more than beating balls on the range, or sinking putts for hours. Practice must be purposeful and designed to make the most progress in the shortest time. If your child's teaching professional focuses on mechanics and has not taught your child effective practice routines – merely giving him drills is not enough – you can order my supplemental material and CD *Mastery Through Purposeful Practice*. In addition to physical practice, juniors will learn how to prepare and practice mentally for competition.

# ACTION IDEAS

## ACTION IDEA #1
### Track your criticisms of your child.

For each criticism, think about and write down alternative ways to get results using constructive correction. For example: A common parental reprimand is, "You never think before you act." Instead, using constructive correction you might say, "In the future, count to three and think about the consequences before you act." Another example: "You'd forget your head if it weren't attached to your neck." Instead, try constructive correction. "Before you leave the house, make sure you have everything you need."

## ACTION IDEA #2
### Develop a discipline game based on the golf penalty system.

Using the collaborative model, sit down with your child to write the *House and Family Rules Book*. Involve him in determining a penalty for each type of infraction. (In golf, if there is an infraction, the rules official does not negotiate because the rules are written down and it is the responsibility of each player to know the rules, play by the rules and accept the penalties.) Note: Keep it simple. Don't over-do the number of rules and penalties. Focus on those things that are really important to you and to the child's well-being.

## ACTION IDEA #3
### Help your child develop good practice habits.

Order Mastery through Purposeful Practice.

# PART IV:
## WISDOM FROM THE PROS

I asked a number of prominent teaching professionals what advice they would give to parents of talented juniors.

### Johnny Miller

Johnny Miller is included in this section not because he is a teaching professional, but because he is founder of the Utah Junior Golf Association and he and his wife Linda have done such a good job raising four golfing sons. He says the greatest influence in his life was his father.

### Johnny Miller's advice to parents:

✦ A person's first introduction to golf should be a totally positive experience. If it is, before long he will be hooked.

✦ Kids thrive on praise and approval. Instruction should be four parts positive to one part correction. The timing of the correction is crucial – the middle of the round is not the time. You should wait until the child is ready to listen.

✦ Golf can be a wonderful ride for life. However if you are overly domineering, or heavy handed, you may get outstanding performance and results from your 10- or 11-year-old, only to have him turn his back on golf as a teenager.

✦ Anyone can be a good winner, but it is important to learn how to handle adversity and little defeats. ("Golf provides plenty of opportunities to experience constant little defeats." – Dr. Bee)

+ It's important to be able to control emotions such as jealousy and anger.

+ It's good when parents can genuinely enjoy another child's win or performance. This teaches good sportsmanship.

+ Golf is a game that instills character traits such as good citizenship, playing by the rules, respect, sportsmanship, communication skills with many different types of people, and self discipline.

♛

### Jim McLean

Jim Mclean is a familiar name to golfers. He is No. 3 on the list of the 50 best teachers in America. Jim McLean Golf Schools – located in Florida, Michigan and California – are consistently rated among the best in the golf instruction business. Jim is also the founder of the Future Collegiate World Tour (FCWT), one of the premier tours for juniors. He has coached top-ranked juniors and professional tour players. Jim's two sons are golfers. In spite of Jim's expertise, he appreciates the coaching of others. Matt McLean has worked with other swing coaches and with me on his mental game. He now plays on the Wake Forest golf team. Jon McLean has won a number of tournaments and is on the 2004 Rolex Junior All-America team. Jim fully supports them, giving his sons every opportunity to develop their talent and live out their dreams.

### Jim McLean's advice to parents:

+ Some players don't make it because they're playing for their parents, not for themselves. They have to want to play and compete for themselves.

- Stay interested in your child's golf, but over-involvement puts too much pressure them.

- Make sure you get some good quality instruction for your child. However, some kids are over-taught. Talent can be diminished by poor instruction. That has happened to a number of tour players.

- It's good to encourage another sport, preferably a team sport.

- Sometimes too much success comes too early. Other kids can catch up. It's hard to keep being the best.

☙

### Eddie Merrins, "The Little Pro"

Eddie Merrins beat Sam Sneed and Byron Nelson in separate exhibition matches as a 17-year-old junior. He went on to a brief career on the PGA Tour before finding and living his passion as teacher/coach/mentor/wise man. He has been on the list of *Golf* magazine's top instructors for 20 years. As coach of UCLA men's golf team, "The Little Pro," as Merrins is fondly known, took the Bruins to the NCAA championship in 1988 – the first West Coast school to win the title since 1956. As head pro at the Bel-Air Country Club in Los Angeles, Merrins has always been interested in the development of young golfers. The list of his famous students is almost as impressive as his career.

### Comments from "The Little Pro"

- Juniors who were "successful" were self-motivated, rather than pushed by parents.

- Today's parents who smell college scholarships, or a place on the professional tour and fame, have misplaced their roles when they get into the ring with their kids and fight their battles for them. The parent's role is to sit in the front row and be the child's greatest fan. Parents interfere with progress when they get too close to the action, go over every shot, every decision, analyze and criticize.

+ Golf is a game that polices its own. Unlike other sports, the rules are taken very seriously. The rules reward integrity, fair play, sportsmanship, and etiquette. Unfortunately, with the fierce competition now, golf is taking on more of the attributes of other sports which don't punish infractions and in which aggressive behavior has become commonplace.

+ My advice to juniors, "Go for it. Compete at the highest levels within the rules. Always play by the rules with a sense of values."

♚

### Rudy Duran:

Rudy Duran was an assistant pro at Heartwell Golf Park in Long Beach, California when he became Tiger Woods' first teaching pro. They worked together six years until Duran left the area to build his own golf course, The Links in Paso Robles. Duran's passion is working with and developing juniors. He wrote *In Every Kid There Lurks a Tiger* a simple five-step program to teach the fundamentals of golf and how to develop your child's potential.

### Rudy Duran's advice to parents:

+ Some toddlers will show extraordinary gifts for golf, suggesting a genetic superiority in this particular sport. Not many kids can understand the game as 4- or 5-year-olds. Help them develop at their own pace.

✦ Those who work with kids should create an environment of fun.

✦ Create opportunities for success. Success breeds success. (Duran developed a concept of a "personal par." That is different from par for the course. Par for nine holes might be 54 for a child who needs four shots to reach the green; any score lower than 54 is defined as shooting below par.)

✦ When a child finishes a round or tournament the first question to ask is either, "Did you have a good time?" or, "What did you like about your round?" The score should never be the first thing mentioned. If your child didn't like the way he played, ask what he learned, and emphasize that learning something is improving too.

✦ If you are a parent who has a problem with bunkers (or anything else) do not pass that expectation onto your child. You don't want him to worry about bunkers. Kids may have no problem at all with shots or clubs that you have defined as difficult.

✦ Get excited with your child. If he comes in third in a tournament and is happy about that, celebrate with him. Do not express disappointment that he wasn't in first place and don't suggest to him that next time he'll be first – that only diminishes his accomplishment.

♔

**Laird Small**
Laird Small is the Director of the Pebble Beach Golf Academy and on the list of the 50 best instructors in America. He has coached golfers on the PGA, LPGA tours,

and we share a European Tour Champion on our client lists. He also has coached a number of highly ranked juniors. Small advocates a path to mastery, a plan outlined by the coach so the child understands the steps to be taken to his ultimate goal. Once the child has a "global" understanding of the process, the pieces can be put in place. He recommends George Leonard's book, Mastery.

### Comments from Laird Small

+ A child must be raised in an environment of both physical and emotional safety.

+ There needs to be a different measure for a win. The concept "win" should not be limited to a tournament win. A child should be considered a winner if she improves a skill, or successfully learns something new.

+ It's important to get good instruction. However, children should have the freedom to experiment rather than try to craft a perfect swing at too early an age. This thwarts creativity – an important element in competition.

+ Learning should be self-paced. Parents need to allow the child to learn at their own pace, not the parents.'

+ As do most other professionals, Small recommends that young junior golfers also play other sports and become multidimensional before concentrating wholly on golf.

## Dave Gooden

Dave Gooden is head pro at Lakeview Country Club in Harrisonburg, Va. I met Dave in 1997, when he asked me to come to Virginia and work on the mental game with his daughter Kansas, and her cousin Mike, son of Paul Gooden, the golf coach at James Madison University. Kansas at 16 was a serious and successful junior golfer and her cousin Mike had professional aspirations. Kansas did get a scholarship to play college golf, but even though it is the "family business," she is not interested in golf as a career. She is now plays some amateur golf, while preparing to go to law school.

### Dave Gooden's advice to parents:

+ It's is a very fine line to straddle between too much involvement in your child's game and not enough. Parents need to know how to read their own child, to gauge how much involvement the child really wants from the parents.

+ If I had it to do over, golf would not be 24/7. My daughter would play other sports, preferably a team sport, and have other interests. I would expect her to do a little work – either in the pro shop or another job that would teach responsibility. Then she would not take all her opportunities for granted.

+ I would minimize the importance of winning and emphasize that golf is a game.

+ If kids start winning when they are very young, their expectations are too high, (as are the parents'.) They can't keep up the wins or extraordinary performance indefinitely and this is likely to have a negative impact on their self-concept. It's important to teach kids how to lose.

# PART V:
## TRAINING YOUR CHAMPION FOR PEAK PERFORMANCE

### BUILDING SELF-ESTEEM

**Self-esteem is a sense of self-worth, competence, confidence, and personal power. Self-esteem is feeling good about yourself and your ability to positively influence the course of your life.**

When you express love, when you support your child's dreams and teach your child life skills, you are building the self-esteem that produces champions. Every time a parent calls a child a derogatory name, punishes unfairly, ignores or rejects a child, discounts his needs, opinions and accomplishments, then that parent chips away at the child's self-esteem. Constant chipping can reduce something to nothing.

If you continually remind your child of his shortcomings and where he needs to improve or what he needs to work on harder, he will get the feeling that he can't please you. That can easily translate into, "I'm inadequate I am incompetent." And even though his golf scores might indicate otherwise, he'll never believe that he is indeed a good player. Constantly pointing out shortcoming does not contribute to improved performance. Instead it creates questions and doubt, undermines self-esteem and confidence and ultimately results in the erosion of performance.

**Focus on your child's strengths and potential, and what he is doing well. Then you can add training to develop**

**your child's promise. This way, your child will maintain self-esteem, the foundation on which champions are built.**

♔

Jolene Stockton was a talented young golfer who was brought up in an environment that didn't provide the support to develop a champion. At the age of 17, when she was at a low point in her game and self-esteem – "It was so bad I was constantly in tears," she recalls – she met Larry Miller, the father of Johnny Miller. When Jolene talks about Larry Miller, she always respectfully refers to him as "Mr. Miller." Jolene said he was the one responsible for the turnaround in her self-esteem, in her game and her success as a professional golfer.

Mr. Miller was not a golf professional, but he learned how to teach by observing Johnny's lessons from one of the best teachers of his time, John Geertsen. When Mr. Miller met Jolene, he saw her potential and offered to help her. He became her teacher, mentor, inspiration and father figure. "He made everything fun," Jolene says. "He was always positive. Whatever I did, there was something good he could say about it. He used to comment on my shots with, 'Good hit, good shot.' Or, if that wasn't true, he would say, 'Good try.' He called me 'Champ.' If I had a bad round and was down on myself, he would say, 'I haven't changed my mind about you. That just wasn't your best round. You're still a great player.'" This encouragement enabled Jolene to fulfill her potential and eventually play professionally on the Japan LPGA Tour. She is now a teaching professional.

When Jolene's daughter Christina was 14, Johnny Miller invited her to play in the Johnny Miller Junior Tournament in Napa, California. His father was there and watched Christina play. She did not score well. When she finished, Mr. Miller told Jolene, "I don't care what she scored, she's a champion. Look at the way she carries herself, at the way she walks and holds her head up. She's a champ."

"Mr. Miller had a way of making you believe you were a champion," said Jolene. His belief in her become a self-fulfilling prophesy Her daughter Christina, now 17, has a dream of the playing on the LPGA Tour and already has the interest of college coaches. Jolene said, "What Mr. Miller taught me has had an influence on every aspect of my life, including how I treat my children day to day. I'm very grateful that he was a part of my life."

There is an important lesson to learn from these examples. Mr. Miller did not tell Jolene and her daughter that everything they did was good. He was specific. There is a school of thought that suggests children be complimented for every effort, even if that effort is inadequate. When you try to build self-esteem by telling a person she did a great job and she knows that is not true, she will not trust your opinions. A child must learn to discriminate between good behavior and performance and that which doesn't measure up to her abilities. Make it a point to praise only the good behavior or performance you want to encourage. Larry Miller's "Good hit" (the hit was good but the shot didn't make it) and "Good try" (you tried but didn't hit a good shot) were brilliant ways to encourage and build self-esteem. However, if not even the try is good, say nothing.

♛

Larry Miller wrote letters to his grandchildren giving them guidelines to live by. Johnny reproduced one of these letters in the afterward of his book, *I Call the Shots*. The letter is full of wonderful wisdom from a loving, encouraging grandfather. Here is just a small part of it, which deals with the topic of this segment:

*"You must be diligent all of the time, never letting in NEGATIVE thoughts or thinking enter your PSYCHE, for it is here where you will either MAKE IT or fail, and that goes for everyone else. The PSYCHE must always be receiving the VERY BEST thoughts and courage. You CANNOT mix JUNK with good thinking and expect to become a champion, it just cannot be done. Go down the straight road and you can't fail."*

The rest of the letter is about a work ethic, courage, intent and purpose, making it big, fighting back from defeat, respect, good cheer, helping others – all championship attributes. Mr. Miller raised a son, Johnny, who is champion in both golf and a life. All of his grandchildren are champion human beings. What better tribute can a man's teachings have?

♛

**The way you identify your child will become an integral part of her self-image.**

During the first major stage of development (birth to about age 5 or 6) a child has no critical judgment and basically believes everything the parent says about him. The child's experiences during that time have a lifelong impact. I'll use the extremes as examples.

✦ If you treat your child as "crown prince of the household" he is likely to have a self-image as being overly important. You've seen these spoiled kids on the golf course ordering their parents around and treating them and others with lack of respect or generally being bad sports. Unbridled praise can result in life long arrogance.

✦ If you are highly critical of your child's efforts, or if you do everything for the child to make sure it is done right, your child is likely to perceive himself as incompetent. That's the child who calls himself "stupid," or other names when he makes a mistake. It's the child who gives up because he can't do anything right, so why try?

These attitudes and behaviors persist. I've worked with many adults, including tour players, who demean themselves. It's interesting that those golfers who "beat up on themselves" are generally way down on the tour money list.

How do you want your child to perceive himself? As a loser, not good enough, lazy, stupid? Or at the other end, perhaps so good that he has no impetus to improve, or elevate himself? As a good parent you probably want your child to have a healthy sense of self-worth and belief in his ability to be successful and happy in whatever he decides to do.

♛

**Everything one hears, sees or experiences leaves a memory trace in the subconscious. It is important to know what a long-term impact negative messages can have on development and how to avoid undermining your child's self-esteem and performance. It is even more important to know how to embed the right messages in your child's subconscious.**

When I work with people who have a performance block and we explore the cause (sometimes through a hypnotic process) we often find that the origin of the problem is 10, 20 or even 30 years in the past. When I work with problems with the "yips," choking, self-sabotage and similar golf issues, 90 percent of the time I find the cause in a negative emotional experience that has been stored in the subconscious. Sometimes it takes years of smoldering for the full effect of negative emotional experiences to show up. Often these imprints are related to failure or an unhappy experience at school, at home, or in another sport.

♛

**"Sticks and stones may break my bones, but names can never hurt me" is the greatest scam that has been perpetrated by well-meaning individuals who try to minimize emotional pain.**

If you were unfortunate enough to have been called names as a child (and really who hasn't?), I'm sure you remember some of them and the people who called you those names. In some cases these incidents have had a long lasting impact on you and still create feelings of discomfort.

One of my tour clients feels guilt and anxiety when she takes a day off from practice. As a child she was constantly called lazy and told if she took time to play or relax before all her work was done, she would never amount to anything. A professional golfer's work is never done. Intellectually she understands that she works harder than most and that she does get physically and mentally worn out. Yet she still feels lazy and guilty when not practicing.

Another client who had won some tour events began to struggle – something that occurs to all golfers at some point in their career. His impatient father thought that name-calling, criticism and pointing out faults would motivate his son to "work harder." Instead, it brought back childhood memories of similar impatient criticism and served only to erode the player's confidence. Before long, the son became what the father constantly called him – a loser.

Yet another client developed putting yips as a result of his father's furious insults when he missed a three-foot putt to lose a junior tournament.

**Words have power. Choose and use them carefully.**

👑

Teasing might be taken lightly and be fun for mature adults, but a child who is just forming his self-concept often takes the teasing to heart. Never tease a child and then berate him for being sensitive, or for taking things too seriously. He really does believe that what you say about him is true. It's also unwise to embarrass a child in front of others. At a recent tournament the parent of a winner laughingly said to another parent, "You'd never believe a guy that can bomb them down the fairway still sleeps with his baby blanket."

At your age, as a parent, you have had years of enough positive experiences to mitigate other's insulting or demeaning comments. You have developed a strong self-concept and can judge the truth of the insults. And, since your peers have learned social graces, chances are they will keep their negative opinions to themselves – unless of course you are a professional golfer who is fair game for the fans and the media.

Your 15-year-old is in the midst of his adolescent search for self and identity. He does not yet have your collection of successes to give him a strong self-concept. He still is questioning his value. Since you know him better than anyone else, he is likely to internalize whatever you say. On the outside he dismisses you and pretends he is on top of things; on the inside, he does listen and he feels fear and confusion. "My parents are great. They do everything for me. But at times I am really afraid of them," said a 16-year-old competitor. An adult who gave up competition at age 15 added, "Kids are really afraid to talk to parents about their feelings when they lose. That was the worst part, thinking no one would understand how I really felt."

♔

## Use words to build self-esteem

I worked with a PGA touring professional who had lost all confidence and was sliding down the money list. At a low point, he told me about some advice his father gave him on how to improve his performance. "Make a list of your weaknesses so you know what to change." He read me the list he had made. "My putting stinks. My short game is sloppy. I am lazy and don't practice enough. I am head-strong and stubborn. I have to do things my way. I don't manage my time well. I make stupid course management decisions. I haven't had a top 10 finish in six months." I found it telling that these are the exact words his father used when he complained to me about his son.

Though he had heard these insults for years whenever he played poorly, the player was able to contain his feelings most of his life. Being told to write the list and dwell on it was the "straw that broke the camels back." My client dwelt upon on this list, becoming more and more discouraged and self-critical as his doubts grew and his confidence plummeted.

I asked him about the other list – the list of his strong points, his positive attributes. He hadn't made that list. No wonder his performance was poor. He had given no thought energy to what had earned him a place on tour – a brilliant junior and college record and the talent to earn a PGA Tour card. We worked together to make a list of his positive traits and achievements. As he focused on that list he began to perceive himself differently – as the champion that he is.

**When you focus on and reinforce your child's positive attributes, behavior and performance, you build his confidence and self-esteem. The behaviors and performance you compliment will multiply. Focusing on what needs improving and what has not developed yet can undermine self-esteem and, ultimately, performance.**

♔

Too many parents' behavior is what I call short-term behavior. In other words, "My child is a prodigy. He can play well at a young age. That will bring me recognition through him. I will do whatever it takes to make my child a star." This type of parenting does work in the short term. The young player gets recognition, adoration, invitations to play in bigger events and tons of media recognition. In the meantime he misses out on childhood and exploring other activities; his entire self-concept is dependent on his golf performance. This is likely to create huge self-esteem problems when the time comes that his game goes south or others do better in competition than he does. There are far more kids with promise who were pushed too hard too young who disappeared from view, than there are those who continued their extraordinary performance.

Tiger Woods did not turn professional until he had an unprecedented six consecutive USGA championships (three U.S. Junior titles and three U.S. Amateur titles). Casey Wittenberg and Ty Tryon both had massive media coverage as teens, even though they had no significant track record of wins. They turned pro at 20 and 17, respectively, struggled mightily, suffered disappointment and now regret their premature attempts at playing the "big tour." They both must rebuild eroded self-confidence and esteem. Contrast this with Aree Song and Paula Creamer, both of whom had a long track record of wins before turning pro in their teens.

**A wise parent discourages his child from getting in over his head and suffering frustration and defeat. The wisest parent values the child for who she is and not her performance on the golf course.**

"It doesn't matter how she plays, if she wins or if she doesn't we react the same. If she wants to stop playing golf, it won't matter to us. She is a good girl. We just want her to be happy," said Mafumi Harrigae, whose daughter Mina won her fourth consecutive California Women's Amateur at the age of 15.

# ACTION IDEAS

## ACTION IDEA #1
### A Self-Esteem Exercise

a. **Ask your child to make a list of his strengths and positive attributes and what he likes about himself.**

b. **You make your own list of what you see as his strong points.**

c. **Discuss these lists as a family. Positives only.**
When I have done similar exercises with people, my results have been the same as those proven in independent research. A person can make a long list of his shortcomings, but the list of positive attributes is generally very short. This is a result of meager affirmative and a lot of critical input when growing up. It's important for self-esteem to reverse that. Go easy on

the negative, while stressing the child's positive behaviors and attributes.

d. **Combine your lists of positive attributes, and write them on a sheet of paper.**
Give the list an appropriate title like," I'm a great kid," or " I like me because ..." Put the list in a prominent place in the child's bedroom.

e. **Copy that list onto several cards and laminate them.**
Put one into something your child has with him most of the time, like his golf bag or back pack, perhaps one on the bathroom mirror. Be sure to carry one yourself to remind you of your blessings. After he really believes the good list – and this may take a few weeks – you can start an "Opportunities for Improvement" list, or the "Next Step" list." This list will be much shorter because you can write down only one thing at a time. For example, if your child loses things or does not take care of them, you can work together to determine an action plan for improvement. When improvement has occurred (It doesn't have to be 100 percent, nothing is perfect) and the child feels successful, you can write down one more opportunity for improvement. This might include one golf performance "Next Step." Each child will have his own "Opportunity for Improvement" list and as each issue is handled, the success will raise his level of self-esteem. That's what you want – a child who feels good about himself.

## ACTION IDEA #2
### The Next Step

When working with juniors I prefer the concept of the "Next Step." When you work on game improvement, focusing on improvement implies to the subconscious: "It's (or I'm) not good enough." The phrase "not good enough" is not likely to enhance confidence and esteem. It often leads to trying too hard, and then to frustration. When there is work still to be done (and when isn't there?) it's best to express satisfaction with what the child has already accomplished. Or as Rudy Duran puts it, "celebrate success," however small. This will enhance self-esteem. Instead of then saying, "You still need to improve distance control with chipping," which suggests "not good enough," tell your child, "You have come a long way, you're are playing really well. Now you are ready for the 'Next Step,' distance control with chipping."

♛

## BALANCING MIND AND BODY

A perfect swing and a strong body do not guarantee a low score. There must be a balance between mind and body. When juniors are trained to use their mind power to supplement their physical game, there is no stopping them. Annika Sorenstam was trained as a member of the Swedish National team. This team had extensive mental training – which is evidenced by Annika's superior performance throughout her career. I had the opportunity to speak to Pia Nilsson, Annika's coach when we both attended the World Scientific Congress of Golf at St Andrews in 1998. We talked about training techniques used to elicit superior performance. These techniques included far more than learning the mechanics of the swing. They also involve going "inward" – learning to be sensitive to the mind and the body's messages.

When mental messages are incompatible with peak performance ("I'm not hitting solid" ... "I'm not confident in my swing today" … " I can't do anything right" … "Dad looks like he's getting mad") it's important to have tools to bring mental messages into line with desired results.

There are a number of techniques that are effective in giving positive messages to the mind that will constructively impact the body and results. Basically, they all are a form of hypnosis or self-hypnosis. Earl Woods said that no one is more mentally prepared than his son. At age 13, Tiger began training with hypnosis and learning self-hypnotic techniques from Jay Brunza.

Contrary to some viewpoints, hypnosis is not "weird." It does not put you under the control of someone else; it actually is way of increasing self-control. It puts a damper on fears and doubts, improves confidence and focus and helps eliminate blocks to peak performance. It is a very natural state. You have experienced it often. When you driving deep in thought and you miss your freeway exit, you have been in road hypnosis – but your driving has been safe. When you are so engrossed in the Super Bowl or a spellbinding movie that you don't hear your partner asking a question, or when you were so involved in a project that you lost track of time, you had slipped into a hypnotic state. You were so focused and "into" the experience that you were able to block out all distractions. Think of how handy that would be on the golf course. As a matter of fact, the "zone" is a light hypnotic trance.

**Hypnosis (and self-hypnosis) is merely the acceptance of suggestion by the subconscious mind. Hypnosis and self-hypnosis can be used to speed learning and also to "unlearn" negative memory traces that interfere with performance.**

In the hypnotic state the mind and body are relaxed and in harmony. When the mind and body are relaxed, brain waves slow down. When this occurs the subconscious can be accessed and it will accept suggestions. Positive change is faster and more permanent and performance is enhanced in this state. There is a massive body of research behind this assertion (see references).

**What this means for you and your child is that when he is relaxed and focused he will learn faster and retain the learning longer than when he is frustrated, under pressure, trying too hard, or stressed in any other way. In addition, when he is relaxed over the ball, his swing will be tension free, leading to a better swing.**

♛

When positive emotions are associated with experiences they are strongly embedded in the subconscious. Paula Creamer's dad said her early teacher rewarded good shots with candy. Larry Miller used positive emotionally charged comments to embed confidence into his students.

The bad news is that negative emotions associated with an experience are more strongly embedded in the subconscious than the positive. These negative embedded emotions are at the root of performance problems – like Beth Daniel's putting yips on Bermuda grass, which were the result of a missed short putt that cost her the 1981 U.S. Open. A lifelong phobia can come from one highly charged frightening experience.

However, there's more good news. Through the use of hypnotic techniques these negative experiences can be neutralized and "reprogrammed" to lose their impact.

♛

Lets look at how this information can be useful to you as

you parent your champion. You already know that learning takes place through repetition – that's the point of practicing, or studying for exams. If this repetition takes place when the subconscious is engaged, the leaning will be incorporated more thoroughly and quickly.

✦ Your child should be in the relaxed heightened focus state when he is learning or practicing. This is hard for him to do if you are "up tight," putting him under pressure and evaluating him critically.

✦ It is even more important for your child to be in the relaxed heightened focus state in competition. This will be almost impossible if you expect too much from him or if he can see your disapproving face and body language as he is lining up his second putt.

✦ When teaching your child anything, remember that rewards are the fastest way to get positive results (verbal rewards are very effective).

✦ Punishment or pain can get results too. However the positive impact is short lived. In the long run, embedding painful memories is going to have a long-term detrimental effect. Pressure and criticism, especially harsh words are bound to sabotage your intent.

♛

**What you think about and talk about becomes your reality.**

What does your family talk about in your home? What thoughts does your child have in his head? Adapt the ideas in this book so that your environment becomes one in which champions are built and nourished. May you and your family enjoy the game of golf and the game of life.

# ACTION IDEAS

**Learn and use relaxation and stress-management techniques. Teach them to your child.** This will head off much of the pre- and post-tournament conflict common in too many families. Your family life will transform. *How to Keep Your Cool* is a CD supplement to this book. You and your junior can listen together.

**Make sure your child has the mental stamina to do her best in competition in all areas of her life.** *The Mental Game for Juniors* CD supplement to this book will introduce your child to some of the basic mental techniques. It includes a segment on self-hypnosis.

# APPENDIX
## TO REMEMBER

*Your life is a reflection of*
*the quality of your thoughts* Dr. Bee

- ✦ A champion is someone who fulfills his potential and lives a life of satisfaction and service. Trophies are a bonus.

- ✦ If you want to raise champion child look at yourself first.

- ✦ You create the footsteps your child will follow in.

- ✦ To love your child means to love him for what he is, not for what you want him to be.

- ✦ They're not finished yet.

- ✦ Keep your "I love you's" up to date.

- ✦ Treat your loved ones like strangers.

- ✦ Whose life is this anyway?

- ✦ There's no percentage in being right.

- ✦ Why find fault? There's no reward offered.

- ✦ The purpose of listening is to learn.

- ✦ There's more to life than golf. There's more to golf than winning.

- ✦ You become what you dwell upon — your child becomes what you label her.

- ✦ Support means to be a rock, a base upon which your child can stand. It doesn't mean pulling him up from above.

+ When you lose your cool, you lose.

+ You will "win" as a parent by recovering from and learning from your mistakes, and not repeating them.

+ A child will be passionate about and self-motivated to fully develop his creative genius.

+ The motivation that leads to achievement comes from within. Sometimes it takes a little stimulation. Sometimes it takes a while to show up.

+ It's the parent's job to maintain discipline. The purpose of discipline is to teach children to make good choices — it is not to inflict pain.

+ Good discipline is proactive, not punitive.

+ Be grateful for the gift of a healthy child.

+ Listening is a sign of respect. When you listen first, you can expect reciprocity.

+ "Seek First to Understand, Then to be Understood."

+ A champion respects all life.

+ Gratitude creates happiness.

+ Communication from you should express your love and support, build your child up, teach him how to achieve his potential, instill values and prepare him to be a champion.

+ When you focus on faults you multiply and magnify them.

+ Words have power – choose and use them carefully.

+ You work to make a living. Golf is a game. It is meant to be played.

# REFFERENCES

The following sources will broaden your understanding of the issues discussed in this book, give you some insights into children their development, and make more suggestions for things you can do to offer a championship environment to your family. Here I am not listing magazine articles used in the preparation of this book because the list is so long it would be unwieldy Those I have quoted from in the text have been referenced there.

**McGraw, Dr. Phil**
    *Family First* **– Free Press, 2004 is must reading.**

**Other useful references:**

Benson, Herbert, M.D. and William Proctor
    *The Break-Out Principle* – Scribner, 2003

Bradley, Michael J. Eddy
    *Yes, Your Teen is Crazy* – Harbor Press, 2003

Briles, Dr. Judith
    *Smart Money Moves for Kids* – Mile High Press, 2002

Burwash, Peter
    *Dear Teenager, If You Only Knew*
    Torchlight Publishing, 2000

Conley, Dalton
    *The Pecking Order* – Pantheon Books, 2004

Covey, Sean
    *The 7 Habits of Highly Effective Teens*
    Running Press 2002

Covey, Stephen R.
    *The 7 Habits of Highly Effective People*
    Simon and Shuster, 1989

Duran, Rudy
    *In Every Kid There Lurks a Tiger* – Hyperion, 2000

Dwyer, Dr. Wayne
    *The Power of Intention* – Hay House, 2004

Epstein-Shepherd, Bee, Ph.D.
    *Mental Management for Great Golf: How to Control Your Thoughts and Play Out of Your Mind*
    Becoming Press, 1996

Garfield, Charles, Ph.D.
*Peak Performance: Mental Training Techniques of the World's Greatest Athletes* – Warner Books, 1984

Gladwell, Malcolm
*Blink* – Little, Brown and Company, 2004

Gookin, Sandra Hardin
*Parenting for Dummies* – IDG Books Worldwide, 1995

Kroger, Otto and Janet M. Thuesen
*Type-Talk* – Delacorte Press, 1988

McCord, Robert
*The Quotable Golfer* – The Lyons Press, 2000

McKay, Matthew, Ph.D. and Patrick Fanning
*Self-Esteem* – New Harbinger Publications, 1987

Miller, Johnny
*I Call The Shots* – Gotham Books, 2004

Murphey, Dr. Joseph
*The Power of Your Subconscious Mind*
Bantam Books,1963

Ostrander, Sheila and Lynn Schroeder
*Superlearning* – Delacorte Press, 1979

Rosenfeld, Alvin, M.D. and Nicole Wise
*The Over-Scheduled Child* – St. Martin's Griffin, 2000

Strege, John
*Tiger: A Biography of Tiger Woods* – Broadway Books, 1997

Tobias, Cynthia Ulrich
*The Way They Learn* – Tyndale House Publishers, 1994

Tofler, Ian, M.D.
*Keeping Your Kids Out Front Without Kicking Them From Behind: How to Nurture High-Achieving Athletes, Scholars and Performing Artists* – Jossey-Bass, 2000

Willis, Mariaemma, M.S. and Victoria Kindle Hodson, M.A.
*Discover Your Child's Learning Style*
Three Rivers Press, 1999

# MY BACKGROUND

*I define myself as a performance, or mental skills coach. I train people to achieve peak performance. Peak performance is a result of a healthy self-concept, goals, a work ethic and then a set of skills that are acquired through practice and diligence. I teach my clients the mental skills proven effective by Olympic and elite athletes and exceptional performers in every field. I have a B.A. in Psychology. My M.A. and my Ph.D. are in Industrial Psychology — the psychology of the work environment — focusing on motivation, communication and training. I also have a doctorate in clinical hypnotherapy. My specialty is hypnosis for performance improvement. I specialize in golf because it is the most intellectual and psychological sport, and I love solving the puzzle of the underlying causes of performance blocks. All my degrees required extensive research into human behavior.*

*During my 30 years as a professional I have worked with people ranging in age from 5 to 85. During my years teaching peak performance in business I trained more than 250,000 people in more than 450 cities internationally. I have learned from books, my students, clients and my colleagues, many of whom are experts in and have written books on human behavior. I have worked with and have interviewed hundreds of golfers, juniors, parents, teaching and touring professionals, caddies, journalists and others in the industry.*

*I have three children and two step-children — all of them married. By the time you read this, I will have a total of 15 grandchildren ranging in age from infants through 17. I have the advantage and privilege of observing the families in action. I also have the joy of playing with the children, and can leave the responsibility and discipline to the parents.*

*The roots of this book go back more than 20 years, when two of my children were competitive ranked junior tennis players. As a parent whose children now have children of their own, I have the opportunity to see the results of my parenting behavior reflected in them. My children are champion human beings. They have been able to forgive their parents' mistakes and learn from them as they parent. Of course when I was in the midst of doing my best with the limited information that I had at the time, or my instincts, I was in constant turmoil as to whether I was doing the right things to raise my children to be responsible, mentally healthy, contributing members of society. Today, even with more expert information than anyone can possibly process, good parents still ask, "Am I doing too much, not enough? ... What is the right thing for my child?" Each child is a unique human being, a combination of innumerable influences. But if you teach your child life skills with love while you support their dreams, you will have done your job.*

Dr. Bee Epstein-Shepherd
Carmel, California, April 2005

# ORDER PAGE

**Give your kids more than lessons and good equipment. Give them the competitive edge with skills that will have a life-long positive impact on every aspect of their lives.**

## BUILDING CHAMPIONS: SUPPLEMENTAL PRODUCTS

**Item #BC 1: How to Find More Time in No Time for Young People.** Time management and life balance skills includes setting goals, prioritizing and other essential organizational skills to help young people manage their heavy school, practice, play and social schedules. This CD and sample scheduling sheets teach skill sets that will have a life-long positive impact.                                            **$29.95**

**Item #BC 2: How to Keep Your Cool.**
Relaxation, stress management and anger management skills that are especially useful for golf but easily transfer to all areas of life. Great for the whole family. Put this CD on your Ipod.                          **$29.95**

**Item #BC 3: Mastery Through Purposeful Practice.**
This CD teaches techniques that are designed for maximum learning and retention. It includes training in the mental rehearsal technique that is used by Olympic and elite athletes in every sport. The additional Practice Tracking sheets can be used as templates.                           **$29.95**

**Item #BC 4: The Mental Game for Juniors.**
Jack Nicklaus said that golf is 90% mental yet the mental game is really neglected by 90% of the golfers. This CD includes mental basics that are guaranteed to improve anyone's performance. As a bonus, it includes a simplified version of the self-hypnotic techniques used by several of the world's best golfers.                                           **$29.95**

**Item #BC 5: The complete set** (Save more than $20.00)  **$99 .00**

**Item #MM 1: Mental Management for Great Golf: How to Control Your Thoughts and Play Out of Your Mind.**
This is the classic book on the mental game. Top tour players, including Major Champions have worked with Dr. Bee as a result of reading this book.                                                        **$25.00**

**Item #MMS 2: The Mental Mastery for Great Golf System.**
A complete system that teaches the mental game. A manual and audiocassette system that includes 16 mental training messages. For a complete description go to www.DrBee.com                          **$389.00**

**Order on line at www.DrBee.com or
by phone (800) 347-6828
For information on personal consultation call
Dr. Bee in California at 831 625-3188**